WORKBOOK

Math for Financial Literacy

SECOND EDITION

Chris Gassen
Faircourt Valuation Investments
Grosse Pointe Woods, MI

Todd Knowlton
Smooth Fusion, Inc.
Lubbock, TX

Publisher
The Goodheart-Willcox Company, Inc.
Tinley Park, IL
www.g-w.com

Copyright © 2023
by
The Goodheart-Willcox Company, Inc.

All rights reserved. No part of this work may be reproduced, stored, or transmitted in any form or by any electronic or mechanical means, including information storage and retrieval systems, without the prior written permission of The Goodheart-Willcox Company, Inc.

ISBN 978-1-64925-508-2

2 3 4 5 6 7 8 9 – 23 – 26 25 24 23 22

The Goodheart-Willcox Company, Inc. Brand Disclaimer: Brand names, company names, and illustrations for products and services included in this text are provided for educational purposes only and do not represent or imply endorsement or recommendation by the author or the publisher.

The Goodheart-Willcox Company, Inc. Safety Notice: The reader is expressly advised to carefully read, understand, and apply all safety precautions and warnings described in this book or that might also be indicated in undertaking the activities and exercises described herein to minimize risk of personal injury or injury to others. Common sense and good judgment should also be exercised and applied to help avoid all potential hazards. The reader should always refer to the appropriate manufacturer's technical information, directions, and recommendations; then proceed with care to follow specific equipment operating instructions. The reader should understand these notices and cautions are not exhaustive.

The publisher makes no warranty or representation whatsoever, either expressed or implied, including but not limited to equipment, procedures, and applications described or referred to herein, their quality, performance, merchantability, or fitness for a particular purpose. The publisher assumes no responsibility for any changes, errors, or omissions in this book. The publisher specifically disclaims any liability whatsoever, including any direct, indirect, incidental, consequential, special, or exemplary damages resulting, in whole or in part, from the reader's use or reliance upon the information, instructions, procedures, warnings, cautions, applications, or other matter contained in this book. The publisher assumes no responsibility for the activities of the reader.

The Goodheart-Willcox Company, Inc. Internet Disclaimer: The Internet resources and listings in this Goodheart-Willcox Publisher product are provided solely as a convenience to you. These resources and listings were reviewed at the time of publication to provide you with accurate, safe, and appropriate information. Goodheart-Willcox Publisher has no control over the referenced websites and, due to the dynamic nature of the Internet, is not responsible or liable for the content, products, or performance of links to other websites or resources. Goodheart-Willcox Publisher makes no representation, either expressed or implied, regarding the content of these websites, and such references do not constitute an endorsement or recommendation of the information or content presented. It is your responsibility to take all protective measures to guard against inappropriate content, viruses, or other destructive elements.

Image Credits. Front cover: file404/Shutterstock.com; Mix Tape/Shutterstock.com. Chapter openers: ideldesign/Shutterstock.com

Introduction

This workbook is designed for use with *Math for Financial Literacy*. Using this workbook will reinforce the concepts you learned in the text as well as provide enrichment activities to improve your communication skills.

Each chapter is organized into three sections: Chapter Review, Chapter Activities, and Project-Based Activity. After reading the corresponding chapter in the text, complete as many exercises as you can without referring to the text. When you have completed the activities, then compare your answers to the information in the text to measure what you have learned.

The *Math for Financial Literacy* workbook is an effective self-assessment tool to prepare you for more formal assessment that your instructor may assign.

Contents

Unit 1
Earning Money and Getting Paid

Chapter 1
Ways to Earn Money..1
Part 1: Chapter Review... 1
Part 2: Chapter Activities.. 5
Part 3: Project-Based Activity.. 7

Chapter 2
Understanding Your Paycheck..11
Part 1: Chapter Review... 11
Part 2: Chapter Activities.. 15
Part 3: Project-Based Activity.. 19

Chapter 3
Income Taxes..21
Part 1: Chapter Review... 21
Part 2: Chapter Activities.. 25
Part 3: Project-Based Activity.. 28

Unit 2
Banking, Purchasing, and Budgeting

Chapter 4
Banking Basics..29
Part 1: Chapter Review... 29
Part 2: Chapter Activities.. 33
Part 3: Project-Based Activity.. 35

Chapter 5
Making Purchases 37
Part 1: Chapter Review.. 37
Part 2: Chapter Activities.. 41
Part 3: Project-Based Activity.. 45

Chapter 6
Budgeting 49
Part 1: Chapter Review.. 49
Part 2: Chapter Activities.. 53
Part 3: Project-Based Activity.. 56

Unit 3
Credit, Debt, and Major Purchases

Chapter 7
Credit Cards 59
Part 1: Chapter Review.. 59
Part 2: Chapter Activities.. 63
Part 3: Project-Based Activity.. 65

Chapter 8
Loans 67
Part 1: Chapter Review.. 67
Part 2: Chapter Activities.. 71
Part 3: Project-Based Activity.. 74

Chapter 9
Housing 77
Part 1: Chapter Review.. 77
Part 2: Chapter Activities.. 81
Part 3: Project-Based Activity.. 84

Chapter 10
Automobiles 87
Part 1: Chapter Review.. 87
Part 2: Chapter Activities.. 91
Part 3: Project-Based Activity.. 93

Unit 4
Building and Protecting Wealth

Chapter 11
Building Wealth..95
   Part 1: Chapter Review..95
   Part 2: Chapter Activities.......................................99
   Part 3: Project-Based Activity..................................101

Chapter 12
Insurance..103
   Part 1: Chapter Review..103
   Part 2: Chapter Activities......................................107
   Part 3: Project-Based Activity..................................110

Chapter 13
Financial Planning..113
   Part 1: Chapter Review..113
   Part 2: Chapter Activities......................................117
   Part 3: Project-Based Activity..................................120

Ways to Earn Money

Name _____ Date _____ Period _____

Part 1: Chapter Review

Multiple Choice

Choose the letter of the correct answer to each question.

1. _____ Money is a tool used primarily to make what easier?
   A. Trading one thing of value for another
   B. Finding a job
   C. Earning minimum wage
   D. Becoming an employer

2. _____ Which of the following are ways you can be paid by your employer?
   A. Hourly wages
   B. Salary
   C. Commission
   D. All of the above.

3. _____ Most employers are required by law to pay employees at least how much per hour?
   A. Minimum commission
   B. Minimum wage
   C. Living wage
   D. Regular earnings

4. _____ Gross pay equals annual salary plus
   A. bonuses.
   B. regular earnings.
   C. double time.
   D. deductions.

5. _____ How many times are employees paid each year if the pay period is semimonthly?
   A. 52
   B. 26
   C. 24
   D. 12

Copyright Goodheart-Willcox Co., Inc.
May not be reproduced or posted to a publicly accessible website.

6. _____ Which of the following will *not* affect the amount of commission earned by a salesperson?
   A. Item price
   B. Base salary
   C. Commission rate
   D. Number of items sold

7. _____ Which of the following is false regarding an independent contractor?
   A. Sometimes called a freelancer or consultant
   B. Works according to a contract
   C. Can be paid by the hour
   D. Cannot be paid by the hour

8. _____ Unearned income could include earnings from
   A. investments.
   B. salary.
   C. bonuses.
   D. commissions.

9. _____ Which of the following is true regarding a contract?
   A. It defines an agreement between two entities.
   B. It cannot be oral.
   C. It can only be used by an independent contractor that does not have unearned income.
   D. It cannot be used by a company which pays minimum wage.

10. _____ When an employee is paid using the straight commission method, the employee receives
    A. only commission.
    B. commission and a base salary.
    C. commission and bonuses.
    D. commission and overtime.

Chapter 1   Ways to Earn Money

Name _____

Fill in the Blank

Using the terms provided, choose the correct answer for each statement.

bartering
commission
gross pay
independent contractor
minimum wage

money
overtime
pay periods
salary
unearned income

1. Larry swaps his used car for a new motorcycle. This is an example of _____.

2. Larry sells his used car for $3,000. Then he spends the $3,000 for a new motorcycle. This transaction uses _____ as a means of exchange.

3. Larry worked 60 hours last week. He was paid his regular wage for the first 40 hours and 1.5 times his regular hourly wage for the extra 20 hours. The extra pay Larry earned is called _____.

4. Larry earned a $25,000 annual salary last year, and he was also paid a $5,000 bonus. The total of these payments is Larry's _____.

5. Most employers are required by law to pay employees at least the _____.

6. Larry is paid each week. His sister is paid once a month. These time frames are called _____.

7. Larry's brother is a commercial electrician who is frequently called and hired by several different companies to do repair work. He would be called a(n) _____.

8. Interest income from a bank savings account is an example of _____.

9. Larry's cousin sells computer software. She is paid a(n) _____ that is a percentage of her total sales.

10. Larry's friend, Gina, is paid $3,000 a month to manage a sandwich shop. This fixed compensation is called a(n) _____.

Copyright Goodheart-Willcox Co., Inc.
May not be reproduced or posted to a publicly accessible website.

Open Response

Answer each of the questions that follow.

1. What is the difference between bartering and using money?

   _____
   _____
   _____
   _____

2. Will your pay period determine how much money you earn in a year? Explain your answer.

   _____
   _____
   _____
   _____

3. What is one advantage of being paid an hourly wage rather than a salary?

   _____
   _____
   _____
   _____

4. Why might an employee want to be paid with a combination of salary and commission, rather than only commission?

   _____
   _____
   _____
   _____

5. What is the difference between earned and unearned income?

   _____
   _____
   _____
   _____

Chapter 1   Ways to Earn Money   5

Name _____

Part 2: Chapter Activities

Section 1.1 Earning by the Hour

Jamie Pries can drive one of his dad's cars, but he must pay $120 each week to cover expenses for gas, maintenance, and insurance. He needs a job to earn the money, but he can't work more than 20 hours a week because he is still in school.

A. If Jamie works 20 hours a week, what is the minimum hourly wage he must earn to cover his expenses?

B. Jamie decides he can only work 16 hours each week because he needs more time for homework. How much will he have to earn each hour to cover his expenses?

C. Jamie is offered a job to work 16 hours each week at the circulation desk of the local library for $11 an hour. He also decides to give the car back to his Dad so that he can save all of his earnings for college! How much can he save after one year?

Section 1.2 Earning a Salary

Shane is a lifeguard at a water park in Florida, and she works 60 hours each week. She earns $12.30 an hour plus time-and-a-half for every hour worked over 40 hours per week. Shane's boss notices that she is a very hard worker and offers her a supervisor job. This is a salaried position that pays $800 weekly with no extra pay for overtime. Shane knows she will probably have to work 60 hours each week to handle the responsibilities of this job.

A. How much does Shane earn per year as a lifeguard?

B. How much will Shane earn per year if she accepts the promotion to supervisor? Would you take the promotion to supervisor if you were Shane? Why or why not?

C. Shane's boss tells her that good supervisors at the company are often promoted within a few years to assistant park manager, and that she could eventually become a park manager! Assistant managers are paid a $2,500 bi-weekly salary. How much would Shane earn per year as an assistant park manager?

D. Park managers earn $4,250 semimonthly plus a $10,000 year-end bonus. How much would Shane earn per year as a park manager? Do you think Shane should accept the promotion to supervisor? Why or why not?

_____

_____

_____

Section 1.3 Other Ways to Earn

A newspaper has five sales representatives. They are listed in the following table, along with sales data from last year. Each representative is paid an annual salary of $20,000 plus 10% commission on subscription sales.

Representative	Subscription Sales
Linda Kent	$42,000
Chuck Olsen	$59,000
Ken Lane	$73,000
Paula White	$90,000
Larry London	$128,000

A. Calculate the commission and annual gross pay that each sales representative earned last year.

_____

_____

_____

_____

_____

_____

B. The newspaper decides to start a new pay system. Sales representatives now earn a 20% commission on subscription sales but only a $10,000 annual base salary. Which representatives will earn a higher annual gross pay under this new system? Which ones will earn a lower annual gross pay?

_____

_____

C. Ken Lane's goal is to earn a $40,000 annual gross pay. How much will he need to have in subscription sales if he is paid a $10,000 annual salary plus a 20% commission?

_____

Chapter 1 Ways to Earn Money   7

Name _____

Part 3: Project-Based Activity

Jimmy browsed through the website of Madison Circle Gardens, which is a sports arena that hosts professional basketball and hockey games throughout the year. He clicked on a page that listed several job openings (shown in the following table). Next to each position is a classification: hourly, salary, or independent contractor. Hourly employees are paid time-and-a-half for any hours worked over 40 in a week. Salaried employees receive fixed compensation and are not paid overtime, but they can receive commission. Independent contractors are hired by Madison under contract but are not employees.

Position	Classification	Compensation
1. Parking Attendant	Hourly	$9.75 per hour
2. Food Service	Hourly	$10.00 per hour
3. Shipping Clerk	Hourly	$10.25 per hour
4. Maintenance	Hourly	$11.00 per hour
5. Merchandising Assistant	Salary	$1,000 semimonthly
6. Merchandising Manager	Salary	$1,500 semimonthly
7. Ticket Sales	Salary	$1,200 monthly plus commission
8. Assistant General Manager	Salary	$4,500 monthly plus $10,000 annual bonus
9. General Manager	Salary	$6,000 monthly plus $30,000 annual bonus
10. Advertising Consultant	Independent Contractor	$50.00 per hour

1. Calculate the regular weekly earnings for each of the four hourly positions. Assume the employees work 40 hours each week.

   _____

   _____

2. Parking attendant and food service workers can volunteer to work 50 hours each week if they want to earn more money. Recalculate the total weekly earnings for these jobs to include the overtime hours. What happens to the average hourly wage for each job when the workweek goes from 40 to 50 hours?

   _____

   _____

   _____

3. Jimmy currently has a maintenance job. He is offered a promotion to the position of merchandising assistant.

   A. What is the annual gross pay for each job? If Jimmy wants to earn a higher annual gross pay, should he accept the promotion?

   _____

   _____

   _____

Copyright Goodheart-Willcox Co., Inc.
May not be reproduced or posted to a publicly accessible website.

B. Jimmy learns that the merchandising assistant position is very demanding and usually requires working 60 hours per week. What would be his average hourly wage as a merchandising assistant if he works 60 hours each week? How might this affect his decision?

_____

_____

_____

C. Jimmy learns that Madison Circle Gardens often promotes employees that work hard and perform well. Merchandise assistants have a good chance to become assistant general managers and, possibly, a general manager. What would be Jimmy's annual gross pay (salary and bonus) as an assistant general manager? How might this affect his decision?

_____

_____

_____

4. Jimmy is curious about the ticket sales position. These employees sell season tickets and ticket packages to large groups. They are paid a base salary of $1,200 a month plus a commission on ticket sales. The commission rate is based on the type of ticket sold as shown in the following table.

Ticket	Commission Rate
General admission	5%
Box seats	6%
Luxury suites	8%

Last year, salespeople at Madison averaged the following sales:

Ticket	Average Sales
General admission	$200,000
Box seats	$150,000
Luxury suites	$100,000

A. What will be Jimmy's annual gross pay if his sales match the average? Compare this to the annual gross pay of the merchandising manager. Which one is higher?

_____

_____

_____

Chapter 1   Ways to Earn Money

Name _____

B. Jimmy is still interested in the ticket sales position, but he is not sure if his ticket sales will match the average. He looks at the ticket sales last year of the highest and lowest ranking salespeople. (See the table that follows.) Suppose Jimmy is confident he can sell as much as the best salesperson. What will be his annual gross pay? What will be his annual gross pay if his sales only match the lowest ranked salesperson?

Ticket	Highest Sales	Lowest Sales
General admission	$300,000	$90,000
Box seats	$250,000	$80,000
Luxury suites	$200,000	$40,000

_____
_____

5. Madison Circle Gardens is currently looking for an advertising consultant to work on a promotional campaign for the upcoming basketball season. This is a 200-hour project that pays $50 per hour.

   A. How much will this consulting job pay?

   _____

   B. Suppose you work as a consultant and charge $50 per hour. How much could you potentially earn each year if you could get hired every week for 40 hours? How much could you potentially earn each year if you could get hired every week for 50 hours?

   _____
   _____

6. What is the annual gross pay of the general manager? This job is one of the highest paying at Madison Circle Gardens. However, it is one of the most demanding jobs and requires working 70 hours a week! What is the average hourly wage of the general manager?

   _____
   _____

Copyright Goodheart-Willcox Co., Inc.
May not be reproduced or posted to a publicly accessible website.

Notes

2 Understanding Your Paycheck

Name _____ Date _____ Period _____

Part 1: Chapter Review

Multiple Choice

Choose the letter of the correct answer to each question.

1. _____ Fred earns $10 an hour as a library assistant. If he worked 40 hours last week, his paycheck would be
   A. equal to $400.
   B. less than $400.
   C. more than $400.
   D. found in a tax table.

2. _____ For which of the following would an employer withhold money from an employee's pay?
   A. Federal income tax
   B. Social Security tax
   C. Medicare tax
   D. All of the above.

3. _____ Which of the following does *not* influence the amount of your federal tax withholding?
   A. The amount you earn
   B. Your health insurance benefits
   C. Your marital status
   D. Your number of dependents

4. _____ A flat-rate tax
   A. means the same tax rate is used for all income levels.
   B. means everyone pays the same amount of tax.
   C. is really the same as a progressive tax.
   D. is used to determine your federal income tax.

5. _____ Which of the following would *not* be an employee benefit?
   A. Health insurance
   B. Paid time off
   C. Retirement plan
   D. Annual salary

6. _____ A W-4 form is used to
   A. apply for minimum wage salary.
   B. calculate federal withholding.
   C. file federal income tax.
   D. calculate Social Security tax.

7. _____ The total annual value of a job is equal to
   A. annual gross pay.
   B. annual gross pay plus Social Security.
   C. annual gross pay plus total annual benefits.
   D. annual gross pay minus total annual benefits.

8. _____ Job expenses
   A. are those you must personally pay because of a job.
   B. should be considered when evaluating a job offer.
   C. could include expenses for commuting and parking.
   D. All of the above.

9. _____ Which of the following is a monetary value of a job?
   A. Flexible work schedule
   B. Annual salary
   C. Opportunity for advancement
   D. Job security

10. _____ Andy's weekly paycheck (after all deductions) is $500. His boss gives him a $100 weekly pay raise. How much will Andy find in his next paycheck?
    A. $300
    B. $600
    C. Less than $600
    D. More than $600

Name _____

Fill in the Blank

Using the terms provided, choose the correct answer for each statement.

deductions
employee benefits
federal withholding
FICA
flat-rate tax

job expenses
monetary values
nonmonetary values
progressive tax
raise

1. Phil noticed that money was withheld from his pay for taxes and some benefits. These withholdings are also called _____.

2. Phil's boss told him he was doing a good job and increased his weekly wage. Phil just got a(n) _____.

3. A deduction from Phil's pay, which was sent to the federal government for federal income tax, is called _____.

4. Because federal income tax is a(n) _____, Phil paid federal tax at a higher rate when his wages increased.

5. Taxes for Social Security and Medicare are part of _____.

6. Phil lives in a state where his state tax rate does not change when his income changes. This is an example of a(n) _____.

7. Phil is offered a job with an annual salary of $30,000 and employer-paid benefits of $5,000. These are _____ that Phil can consider when evaluating the offer.

8. In addition to his weekly wage, Phil receives _____ of health insurance and six paid vacation days.

9. Phil is evaluating a job offer and realizes he will need to pay _____ of $100 a week to commute to work and park his car.

10. Phil chose a job with a lower pay because there was better job security and his coworkers were much nicer to work with. These are examples of _____.

Open Response

Answer each of the questions that follow.

1. What are three factors that influence the amount of an employee's federal tax withholding?

   _____
   _____
   _____
   _____

2. Is Social Security tax a progressive tax? Briefly explain.

   _____
   _____
   _____
   _____

3. Does the employer or the employee pay for fringe benefits?

   _____
   _____
   _____
   _____

4. Would you generally prefer to pay for an employee benefit on a pre-tax or after-tax basis? Why?

   _____
   _____
   _____
   _____

5. Will an employee with higher or lower income generally see a greater percentage of a pay raise in their paycheck?

   _____
   _____
   _____
   _____

Name _____

Part 2: Chapter Activities

Section 2.1 Calculating Taxes

The payroll information for five instructors at the Hai Karate Academy is shown in the following table. A portion of the married persons federal withholding table is shown in Figure 2-1.

Employee	Weekly Salary	Marital Status	Withholding Allowances
B. Lei	$609	Married	0
B. Norris	$641	Married	1
J. Lund	$579	Married	2
P. Moreta	$634	Married	3
K. Kato	$591	Married	1

A. Refer to Figure 2-1. What is the federal withholding for each instructor?

MARRIED Persons—WEEKLY Payroll Period
(For Wages Paid through December 20--)

And the wages are—		And the number of withholding allowances claimed is—				
		0	1	2	3	4
At least	But less than	The amount of income tax to be withheld is—				
$550	$560	$43	$33	$25	$18	$11
560	570	45	34	26	19	12
570	580	46	35	27	20	13
580	590	48	37	28	21	14
590	600	49	38	29	22	15
600	610	51	40	30	23	16
610	620	52	41	31	24	17
620	630	54	43	32	25	18
630	640	55	44	33	26	19
640	650	57	46	35	27	20

Source: Department of the Treasury, Internal Revenue Service, Publication 15 (2012)

Figure 2-1.
Excerpt from Married Persons Withholding Table

B. What are the Social Security (tax rate 6.2%) and Medicare (tax rate 1.45%) taxes for each instructor?

C. What is the state tax (flat-rate tax of 4%) for each instructor?

D. What is the net pay (weekly) after all the above deductions for each instructor?

Name _____

Section 2.2 Benefits

The following table shows a list of five employees, along with their hourly wages and weekly work hours. Employees who work at least 32 hours are considered full-time employees and receive health and dental insurance. Health insurance is worth $5,000 annually, and dental insurance is worth $1,000 annually. Full-time employees also receive up to $3,000 each year in tuition reimbursement for college classes they complete successfully. Employees who work fewer than 32 hours are considered part-time employees and do not receive benefits.

Employee	Hourly Wage	Weekly Hours
J. Nasmath	$12.00	40
P. Lemmons	$11.50	40
D. May	$10.75	32
M. Sells	$10.50	24
B. Eubanks	$10.25	24

A. What is the annual gross pay (for 52 weeks) for each employee?

_____
_____
_____
_____
_____
_____

B. What is the annual value of each job?

_____
_____
_____
_____
_____
_____
_____

Section 2.3 Analyzing Pay

Five auto technicians just received pay raises as listed in the following table.

Employee	Hourly Wage	Rate of Raise
A. Bradley	$15.00	3%
B. Chung	$14.00	2%
S. Rodgers	$13.00	3%
F. Harper	$12.75	3%
M. Cortez	$12.50	4%

A. What is the hourly amount of the raise for each employee?

B. What is the new hourly wage for each employee after their raise?

Name _____

Part 3: Project-Based Activity

Mira Thomas just finished browsing a job search website that lists registered nursing positions. She narrowed her search to five jobs in her city as listed in the following table. All are full-time positions in which she would work 40 hours per week.

Employer	Hourly Wage
City General Hospital	$13.50
Southeastern Hospital	$13.65
St. Luke Hospital	$14.00
Welby Clinic	$14.65
Central Clinic	$15.00

1. Calculate the amount Mira will receive in yearly gross pay for each job. Assume she will work 52 weeks per year.

   _____
   _____
   _____
   _____
   _____
   _____

2. Each of the employers also offers a package of fringe benefits. The annual value of these benefits is listed in the following table. Calculate the total annual value of each job. Which job has the highest value?

Employer	Health Insurance	Dental Plan	Disability Insurance	Tuition
City General Hospital	$5,000	$1,000	$1,000	$4,000
Southeastern Hospital	$5,000	$900	$900	$2,000
St. Luke Hospital	$4,000	$900	$700	$40
Welby Clinic	$3,000	$500	$500	$0
Central Clinic	$3,000	$400	$0	$0

   _____
   _____
   _____
   _____
   _____
   _____

3. Suppose Mira is not interested in continuing her education and will not take advantage of the tuition reimbursement benefit. Which job now has the highest total annual value for Mira?

_____

_____

4. Suppose Mira would use the tuition reimbursement option. However, she would not use the health insurance benefit because she is covered under her husband's health insurance. Which job now has the highest total annual value for Mira?

_____

_____

5. Mira realizes that she will need to pay for job expenses such as parking and travel costs. She will also have to pay for childcare for her daughter while she is at work. However, City General and Southeastern offer a flexible work schedule, so she would not need childcare for her daughter. The weekly expenses for each job are shown in the following table. Calculate the total annual expenses for each job. Assume Mira works 52 weeks per year.

Employer	Travel	Parking	Childcare
City General Hospital	$70	$25	$0
Southeastern Hospital	$50	$10	$0
St. Luke Hospital	$50	$0	$200
Welby Clinic	$35	$0	$200
Central Clinic	$45	$0	$200

_____

_____

_____

_____

_____

6. What is the net annual value of each job? Assume that Mira will use all the employee benefits that are offered by each employer. Based on monetary considerations, which job would look most attractive to Mira?

_____

_____

_____

_____

_____

_____

3 Income Taxes

Name _____ Date _____ Period _____

Part 1: Chapter Review

Multiple Choice

Choose the letter of the correct answer to each question.

1. _____ Individuals are required to file a report of their income and the taxes that are owed to the federal government in a(n)
   A. tax table.
   B. W-2 form.
   C. federal tax return.
   D. W-4 form.

2. _____ Which of the following is an example of a federal tax return?
   A. Form 1040
   B. W-2 form
   C. W-4 form
   D. Form 10-K

3. _____ A W-2 form
   A. comes from the state government.
   B. summarizes an employee's earnings and the amounts withheld from the employee's paychecks.
   C. is not needed when filing a federal tax return if you earned hourly wages.
   D. summarizes the employee's itemized deductions.

4. _____ Gross income on a tax return includes which of the following?
   A. Wages
   B. Tax credits
   C. Itemized deductions
   D. All of the above.

5. _____ What is a tax credit?
   A. A form that exempts a person from paying taxes
   B. An amount of money that a taxpayer is allowed to subtract from the taxes owed
   C. The amount of capital gain not subject to tax
   D. A tax break that is not available to single taxpayers

6. _____ What figures are needed to determine taxable income?
   A. Gross income
   B. Adjustments to gross income
   C. Deductions
   D. All of the above.

7. _____ Leonard just completed his tax return which shows he owes $4,800 in tax. His employer withheld $5,000 in federal tax from his paychecks last year. Which of the following is true?
   A. Leonard now needs to pay the federal government $4,800 in tax.
   B. Leonard now needs to pay the federal government $200 in tax.
   C. Leonard can file his return and receive a $200 tax refund.
   D. Leonard can file his return and receive a $5,000 tax refund.

8. _____ Which of the following would result in higher taxable income?
   A. Higher wages
   B. Lower investment income
   C. More tax credits
   D. Higher deductions

9. _____ Self-employed taxpayers
   A. are subject to the federal income tax like everyone else.
   B. are exempt from federal income tax.
   C. are exempt from Social Security tax but not Medicare.
   D. may not deduct any expenses when determining taxable income.

10. _____ Which is true regarding the federal estate tax?
    A. Federal estate tax is essentially the same as a capital gains tax.
    B. Federal estate tax is paid out of the value of the estate before the estate is transferred to an heir.
    C. Federal estate tax will not be paid if the heir is still living.
    D. There is no way to avoid paying federal estate tax because everyone eventually dies.

Name _____

Fill in the Blank

Using the terms provided, choose the correct answer for each statement.

capital gain
estate tax
federal tax return
gross income
self-employment tax

tax deductible
tax refund
tax table
taxable income
W-2 form

1. Each year by April 15, Luanne files a(n) _____, which reports her income to the federal government and determines the amount of tax she owes.

    federal tax return

2. Luanne's _____ last year included $22,700 in wages and $837 in investment income.

    gross income

3. Luanne's employer sent her a(n) _____, which summarizes her earnings and the amount withheld from her paychecks.

    W-2 form

4. The total of your earned and unearned income within a specific period of time is your _____.

    taxable income

5. Luanne made a(n) _____ contribution to a local charity, which she subtracted from her adjusted gross income to determine taxable income.

    tax deductible

6. Luanne received a(n) _____ after determining she owed less in federal tax than her employer withheld from her paychecks.

    tax refund

7. After determining the amount of her taxable income, Luanne found the amount of tax she owed in a(n) _____.

    tax table

8. Luanne realized a(n) _____ last year after selling shares of stock she owned at a profit.

    capital gain

9. Luanne's brother Tony is an independent contractor who pays a(n) _____, which is the equivalent of both an employee and employer FICA contribution.

    self-employment tax

10. Luanne's mother recently passed away. Before Luanne received her inheritance from her mother's estate, a(n) _____ was paid.

    estate tax

Open Response

Answer each of the questions that follow.

1. Your friend Merv tells you he just found the amount of his taxable income on the W-2 form he received from his employer. What is your response?

   _____
   _____
   _____
   _____

2. Could gross income and taxable income be the same on a tax return? Why or why not?

   _____
   _____
   _____
   _____

3. Sherri bought stock in a company on January 2 for $24 a share. Later that year on December 30, the stock was selling at $30. Sherri wanted to sell the stock at a profit, but she was told by a tax advisor to strongly consider waiting a few days. Why?

   _____
   _____
   _____
   _____

4. When should you use a standard deduction on your federal tax return?

   _____
   _____
   _____
   _____

5. Why do many estates never pay estate tax?

   _____
   _____
   _____
   _____

Part 2: Chapter Activities

Section 3.1 Federal Taxes

The following table shows the monthly salaries and investment income for four employees. The employees' retirement plan payments, which count as a deduction from gross income, are also listed.

Employee	Monthly Salary	Investment Income	Retirement Plan
L. Carson	$4,050	$4,900	$2,430
M. Wong	$4,450	$5,510	$0
J. Connor	$4,500	$3,175	$2,580
R. Perez	$7,590	$6,875	$4,550

A. What is the adjusted gross income of each employee?

_____
_____
_____
_____

B. The following table shows the tax deductible expenses for each employee. Using the adjusted gross income you calculated earlier, find the taxable income for each employee. Each is a single taxpayer and allowed a $12,400 standard deduction.

Employee	Deductible Expenses
L. Carson	$6,900
M. Wong	$13,850
J. Connor	$8,690
R. Perez	$16,050

_____
_____
_____
_____
_____

Section 3.2 Capital Gains Taxes

Rafe has sold some property and stocks. Now he must determine the amount of capital gain or loss for these transactions.

A. Rafe sold a home for $129,900. He bought the home six years ago for $121,000. What is the amount of Rafe's capital gain or loss? Is the gain or loss long-term or short-term?

_____

B. Rafe sold three stocks this year. The proceeds from each sale and the corresponding purchase amounts are shown in the following table. Stocks A and B were purchased this year. Stock C was bought over two years ago. Calculate the capital gain or loss on each sale. Identify each gain or loss as short-term or long-term.

Stock	Sale Proceeds	Purchase Amount
Stock A	$12,311	$20,011
Stock B	$19,204	$8,021
Stock C	$7,908	$8,444

_____

_____

_____

C. What is Rafe's net gain or loss on the three stocks?

_____

Name _____

Section 3.3 Other Income Taxes

The earnings for five self-employed individuals last year are shown in the following table.

Name	Earnings
B. Chin	$39,800
J. Diaz	$49,800
L. Nelson	$51,000
W. Wolf	$68,663
C. Borman	$98,763

A. Calculate the self-employment tax for each person using 15.3% as the tax rate.

_____
_____
_____
_____
_____

B. Suppose Borman earned $148,000 last year. She calculates her self-employment tax by multiplying $148,000 by 15.3%, which equals $22,644. Is Borman correct? Briefly explain.

_____
_____

Part 3: Project-Based Activity

Freddy Bauer is an assistant coach for a minor league hockey team. He just received his W-2 form and is ready to file his federal tax return. In the past, Freddy has used the services of a tax preparer, but he decided to prepare the return himself this year to save some money. He asks you for some help.

1. Freddy's wages last year were $50,700. He earned $493 in interest income from a savings account and $2,400 from a condominium he rented to a friend. Last year, Freddy paid $1,465 into an IRA account, which counts as a deduction from his gross income. What is Freddy's gross income and adjusted gross income?

2. Next, Freddy gives you receipts for some expenses from last year as shown in the following table. You read through the tax rules and tell Freddy that his grocery bill and veterinary expense are not tax deductible. However, the other items can be deducted. Freddy is single and currently is allowed a $12,400 standard deduction. Calculate Freddy's taxable income.

Expense	Amount
Real estate tax	$3,200
Home mortgage interest	$2,500
Charitable contributions	$4,900
State income tax	$3,100
Veterinary bill for cat	$215
Annual grocery bill	$6,313

3. By looking at the appropriate tax table, you find that Freddy's tax due amount is $4,414. His W-2 form shows that $6,205 has already been deducted from Freddy's paychecks last year for federal income tax. Will Freddy receive a tax refund or will he have to pay additional tax? How much?

4. Before Freddy files his return he remembers something. He purchased a rental condominium six years ago for $36,000. He still owns it and estimates that it is probably worth about $45,000. Freddy asks you if he should pay a capital gains tax. What is your opinion?

5. Freddy also remembers that his Uncle Nino gave him a $500 gift last year. Later last year, Uncle Nino passed away, and Freddy received a $28,000 inheritance as his portion of Uncle Nino's estate. Freddy wonders if these amounts should be included as part of his taxable income. What do you think?

4 Banking Basics

Name _____ Date _____ Period _____

Part 1: Chapter Review

Multiple Choice

Choose the letter of the correct answer to each question.

1. _____ What are two main types of accounts at banks?
   A. Checking and balancing
   B. Checking and savings
   C. Checking and debit
   D. Savings and borrowing

2. _____ Interest is a fee charged
   A. by a lender to a borrower.
   B. by a borrower to a lender.
   C. by a bank for writing a check.
   D. by a bank for making a deposit.

3. _____ With an electronic transfer, money is transferred from one account to another without
   A. recordkeeping.
   B. overdraft protection.
   C. service charges.
   D. any check or cash involved.

4. _____ When your check clears the bank, it
   A. has been processed and the money transferred out of your account.
   B. has been inspected and determined to be free of forgery.
   C. is guaranteed for payment by federal deposit insurance.
   D. is eligible to be cashed at a credit union.

5. _____ If you write checks for more money than the amount you have in your checking account, your account
   A. cannot have outstanding transactions.
   B. will be overdrawn.
   C. will be automatically reconciled.
   D. does not meet credit union regulations.

6. _____ Simple interest
   A. cannot be paid by credit unions.
   B. cannot be expressed as a percentage.
   C. is another name for compound interest.
   D. is paid only on the original principal.

7. _____ The current amount of money in your bank account is called the
   A. registered amount.
   B. balance.
   C. deposited amount.
   D. statement.

8. _____ Which of the following are places you can do banking?
   A. Credit union
   B. Bank
   C. Automated teller machine
   D. All of the above.

9. _____ You can use a debit card to
   A. access money in your checking account and transfer it to someone else.
   B. accept a payroll deposit from your employer.
   C. write a check.
   D. get overdraft protection.

10. _____ The purpose of reconciling your bank account is to
    A. convert simple interest to compound interest.
    B. get overdraft protection.
    C. verify that you agree with your bank on the balance.
    D. verity that your account complies with federal law.

Name _____

Fill in the Blank

Using the terms provided, choose the correct answer for each statement.

balance	debit
bank	overdrawn
check	savings account
checking account	service charge
compound interest	statement

1. Kelly needed a safe place to keep her money, so she opened an account at a local _____.
   _____

2. A(n) _____ is a fee a bank charges you for having an account.
   _____

3. Kelly opened a(n) _____ so she would have a convenient way to deposit her weekly paychecks and pay her monthly bills.
   _____

4. Kelly wrote a(n) _____ for $96.23 to pay her monthly cell phone bill.
   _____

5. After Kelly mailed her $96.23 payment to the cell phone company, she looked in her checking account register and discovered her account _____ was only $73.28!
   _____

6. Kelly's $96.23 check was presented to her bank for payment. However, her checking account became _____ because she only had $73.28 in the account.
   _____

7. Kelly paid for her groceries using a(n) _____ card, which authorizes her bank to transfer money to the supermarket's bank account.
   _____

8. Kelly opened a(n) _____ at her bank so she could deposit money each month which would earn interest and be easily available to withdraw.
   _____

9. Kelly's savings account pays _____, where the interest is calculated on the principal and accumulated interest.
   _____

10. Kelly's bank sends her a(n) _____ every month that summarizes her account activity, including all her deposits, withdrawals, and fees.
    _____

Open Response

Answer each of the questions that follow.

1. How do banks make money?

   _____
   _____
   _____
   _____

2. What is the difference between a checking account and a savings account?

   _____
   _____
   _____
   _____

3. People are writing fewer checks than in the past. Why?

   _____
   _____
   _____
   _____

4. Why is it important to maintain an accurate checking account register and reconcile your account periodically?

   _____
   _____
   _____
   _____

5. You want to deposit money in a savings account for three years and are choosing between two banks. Each bank advertises the same interest rate; however, one bank pays simple interest and the other compounds the interest. Which account would you prefer? Why?

   _____
   _____
   _____
   _____

Name _____

Part 2: Chapter Activities

Section 4.1 Opening an Account

Sanjo just received her paycheck. She plans to deposit it and some other checks in her bank account. In addition, Sanjo decides to deposit some money she has been saving in a large jar on her dresser.

A. Sanjo's paycheck is for $198.73. She also has three checks she received for her birthday for $50, $25, and $20. What is the total amount of the checks she plans to deposit?

_____

B. Sanjo empties the jar from her dresser and counts $39.00 in cash and $13.97 in coins. If she deposits the cash and coins along with the checks, what will be the net deposit?

_____

Section 4.2 Checking Accounts

Tina had a $1,371.17 balance in her checking account at Fidelity Bank on May 1. The transactions she had during the rest of the month are shown in the following table.

Date	Transaction
May 3	Deposited tax refund check of $433.39
May 3	Withdrew $80.00 cash from an ATM
May 6	Wrote check #112 to ACE TV for a cable bill of $112.19
May 6	Wrote check #113 to Home Properties to pay rent of $700.00
May 6	Wrote check #114 to Valley Utilities to pay an electric bill of $45.18
May 8	Deposited $125.00 cash
May 15	Wrote check #115 to Star Bank to pay a credit card bill of $833.88
May 17	Deposited paycheck of $733.39
May 18	Withdrew $100.00 cash from an ATM
May 22	Wrote check #116 to Antonio Perez for $25.00 for a birthday gift
May 25	Wrote check #117 to Kenmore Energy to pay a gas bill of $79.88
May 29	Wrote check #118 to Statewide to pay an auto insurance bill of $592.45
May 31	Deposited paycheck of $733.39

A. Record Tina's transactions in the checking account register shown. Calculate her balance after each transaction.

NUMBER	DATE	DESCRIPTION	PAYMENTS	✓	DEPOSITS	BALANCE
	5/1	Balance carried forward				1,371.17

B. What is the total of the deposits Tina made in May? What is the total of the payments and withdrawals Tina made in May? Does the difference in these two amounts plus the balance carried forward equal the ending balance? If not, check your calculations.

_____

_____

Section 4.3 Savings Accounts

Stewart has been saving money for college that he earned at his part-time job. He won't need the money for college for two years. He is considering options for what to do with the money during those two years.

A. Stewart is considering loaning $2,000 to his brother for one year. His brother would repay the loan plus 3% simple interest. How much interest will Stewart receive?

_____

B. Since Stewart will not need his money for college until two years from now, he is considering placing the $2,000 into a savings account at Country Bank. The money would earn 3% interest compounded quarterly. What will be Stewart's savings account balance at the end of two years? How much interest will he earn?

_____

C. Stewart checks with another local bank, City First Bank, and finds that it offers 3.5% compounded quarterly on savings accounts. Suppose Stewart keeps his $2,000 in a savings account at City First Bank for two years. How much more interest will Stewart receive here than at Country Bank?

_____

Name _____

Part 3: Project-Based Activity

Inga Bitterman is a business student at a university where she also works as a graduate assistant. She just received her first paycheck. Inga decided to open a checking account at a credit union that serves university employees. There is no monthly service charge on this account, although there will be a $35.00 fee if the account is overdrawn.

1. Inga makes an initial deposit on October 1, which includes a paycheck for $359.78, a check that was a birthday gift for $50.00, cash totaling $25.00, and coins totaling $4.78. What is Inga's net deposit?

   _____

   _____

2. Inga's transactions during the rest of October are shown in the following table. Record Inga's October 1 opening deposit in the checking account register. Then record her transactions for the rest of the month. Calculate the balance after each transaction.

Date	Transaction
October 2	Withdrew $80.00 cash from an ATM
October 3	Wrote check #100 to Fast Phone to pay phone bill of $47.64
October 4	Deposited birthday gift of $75.00
October 10	Wrote check #101 to University Book Store for $211.74
October 15	Deposited payroll check of $359.78
October 16	Wrote check #102 for $60.00 for football tickets
October 17	Deposited $100.00 rebate check from computer purchase
October 19	Wrote check #103 to Super Food Mart for groceries for $39.43
October 22	Withdrew $40.00 cash from ATM
October 25	Withdrew $40.00 cash from ATM
October 30	Wrote check #104 to Community Fund for charitable contribution for $25.00
October 30	Wrote check #105 to First Bank for car payment of $229.00
October 31	Deposited payroll check of $359.78

NUMBER	DATE	DESCRIPTION	PAYMENTS	✓	DEPOSITS	BALANCE

3. Inga receives her monthly statement from the credit union, and it shows a statement balance of $455.53 as of October 31. Does this amount match the October 31 balance in her checking account register? Should she be surprised if there is a difference?

_____

_____

_____

4. Inga reviews her monthly credit union statement and finds that both checks she wrote on October 30 did not clear. Her paycheck deposit on October 31 also does not yet appear on her credit union statement. Calculate the adjusted balance from her credit union statement.

_____

5. Can you reconcile the balances in Inga's checking account register and the credit union statement?

_____

_____

6. Inga currently has $10,000 deposited in a savings account at Hometown Bank where it earns 2.5% annual interest rate compounded quarterly. However, the credit union offers her a 3.5% annual interest rate compounded quarterly. How much will her deposit be worth after three years at each place? Do you think it will be worth Inga's effort to transfer her savings from Hometown Bank to the credit union?

_____

_____

5 Making Purchases

Name _____ Date _____ Period _____

Part 1: Chapter Review

Multiple Choice
Choose the letter of the correct answer to each question.

1. _____ An example of a market could include
   A. classified ads.
   B. eBay.
   C. a department store.
   D. All of the above.

2. _____ Buyers and sellers meet in a market to exchange
   A. goods but not services.
   B. services but not goods.
   C. goods, services, or information.
   D. credit limits.

3. _____ What does market size refer to?
   A. Size of a store
   B. Impact of advertising
   C. Number of buyers
   D. Number of sellers

4. _____ Sales tax rates and laws
   A. are established only by the federal government.
   B. apply to everything that is purchased.
   C. do not apply when using a credit card.
   D. vary by state and city.

5. _____ Coupons give a discount
   A. before the sales tax is applied.
   B. after the sales tax is applied.
   C. only when there is no sales tax.
   D. only when an item does not have a rebate.

6. _____ What is the potential drawback of purchasing an item based on a rebate?
A. The discount is usually much larger than one given on a coupon.
B. Many people never complete the process to claim the rebate.
C. The rebate is given immediately at the time of purchase.
D. Rebates are not available when you use a credit card.

7. _____ Which is an example of a payment card?
A. Debit card
B. Credit card
C. Gift card
D. All of the above.

8. _____ Which statement is true regarding a credit card?
A. A credit card company pays for a purchase and loans you the money.
B. A credit card is the same as a debit card.
C. A credit card is the same as a gift card.
D. Sales tax does not apply when using a credit card.

9. _____ When making a charge account purchase
A. a debit card is often used.
B. credit limits are rarely involved.
C. the customer promises to pay at a later date.
D. the customer promises to pay at a later date and does not receive the good or service until a later date.

10. _____ Knowing the unit price would be advantageous to a customer when
A. buying a product that comes in different sizes.
B. buying a car.
C. making a layaway purchase.
D. using a credit card.

Name _____

Fill in the Blank

Using the terms provided, choose the correct answer for each statement.

charge account
contract
credit limit
installment plan
market

market size
rebate
sales tax
tip
unit price

1. The _____ for cigarettes has been declining in the United States as the health hazards of smoking have become better known.

2. The _____ for laptop and tablet computers is diverse. They can be purchased at electronics stores, discount stores, online retailers, and directly from the manufacturers.

3. Jack worked as a car park valet and typically received a $2 _____ when he brought out a car to its owner.

4. The 6% _____ in Michigan adds $1,500 to the cost of a new car priced at $25,000.

5. Jerry is a house painter who buys his paint and supplies at a local hardware store on a(n) _____, which he pays in full at the end of every month.

6. The maximum amount you can carry on your charge account is your _____.

7. The total bill for Jeanine's braces was $5,500. Her parents made payments to the orthodontist each month on a(n) _____ over three years.

8. Mike notices that there are four sizes of his favorite brand of peanut butter. He bought the largest size because its _____ was the lowest.

9. Francine bought a laptop computer which she saw advertised for $399. However, this price was after a $100 _____, so she needed to pay $499 plus tax at the store.

10. Marvin signed a(n) _____ to lease his apartment, which specified that he would make $800 monthly payments for one year.

Open Response

Answer each of the questions that follow.

1. Give three examples of markets where you can purchase a bicycle.

2. Identify two differences between a coupon and a rebate.

3. What is an advantage of making purchases on a charge account? Why might a merchant find it advantageous to offer a charge account?

4. What is the difference between the price of an item and its unit price? Why are unit prices useful?

5. What is the risk of locking in a price in a contract? Do you think the risk of locking in a price is greatest for a contract that is for one year, three years, or five years?

Name _____

Part 2: Chapter Activities

Section 5.1 Basics of Purchasing

Candice plans to make several purchases involving coupons and rebates. She will also need to pay sales tax on some items.

A. Candice is checking out at a discount store with the items listed in the following table. She has coupons for a few of them. Some items are exempt from the 6% sales tax. What is the final price of each item before tax? What is Candice's total bill after tax?

Item	Price	Coupon	Exempt From Sales Tax?
Tortilla chips	$2.99	$0.50	Yes
Cola	$3.29	$1.00	Yes
Hockey stick	$49.99		No
Salsa	$2.79		Yes
Ink cartridge	$16.98	$5.00	No
Jeans	$29.49		No
Toothpaste	$2.49	$0.75	No

_____
_____
_____
_____
_____
_____
_____
_____
_____

B. Candice shops for office equipment and supplies at a local electronics store. She has coupons she found online, including one that offers a 5% discount on any two items in the store. There are also rebates available on some items. A list of her purchases is shown in the following table. Candice must pay 6% sales tax on all the items. What is the final cost of each item after coupons, rebates, and sales tax? What is the final cost of her entire purchase after coupons, rebates, and sales tax?

Item	Price	Coupon	Rebate
Computer	$1,000.00	5% off	$100.00
Printer	$199.99	5% off	
Paper	$20.00	$5.00	$5.00
Ink cartridges	$36.97		
Software	$89.00		$20.00

C. Candice stops for lunch at a restaurant and orders a triple-decker bacon buffalo burger, a jumbo milkshake, a brownie sundae, and onion rings. The check is $18.79 before tax. She has a coupon for free onion rings, which were $3.99. Candice got great service and wants to tip 20% of the total check (before the coupon). How much is the tip? What is the total amount of her bill including tip and 6% sales tax?

Chapter 5   Making Purchases   43

Name _____

Section 5.2 Payment Options

Jerry is a professional house painter and buys supplies at a local paint and supply store. On March 1, he opened a charge account with a $1,500 credit limit at the store.

A. Jerry's purchases in March are shown in the following table. What is the total of each purchase after a 5% sales tax?

Date	Item Purchased	Quantity	Unit Price
March 3	Satin paint – gallon size	6	$32.00
March 3	Premium paint brushes	4	$11.99
March 7	Eggshell paint – gallon size	8	$29.00
March 9	Primer – gallon size	3	$19.39
March 11	Exterior paint – gallon size	7	$35.99
March 15	Drop cloths	4	$12.00
March 17	Paint sprayer	1	$179.00
March 24	Waterproof paint – gallon size	10	$24.99

_____
_____
_____
_____
_____
_____
_____
_____

B. What is Jerry's account balance after his March 24 purchase? How much more can he buy without exceeding his credit limit?

_____
_____

Copyright Goodheart-Willcox Co., Inc.
May not be reproduced or posted to a publicly accessible website.

Section 5.3 Influences on Purchasing Decisions

Clarice wants to rent an apartment for two years. She just found one with a one-year lease for $725 a month. However, the owner offers her a deal where she can rent the same apartment with a two-year lease for only $700 a month.

A. How much is the total cost of the two-year lease at $700 per month?

_____

B. How much is the total cost of leasing for two years if Clarice signs a one-year lease at $725 per month and then renews for another year at the same rate?

_____

C. Suppose Clarice signs a one-year lease at $725 a month. After a year she is ready to renew for another year, and she finds that rental rates have dropped. She can now rent her apartment for one year at only $650 a month with the first month free. What will be her total cost of leasing over two years? How does this compare to signing a two-year lease at $700 a month?

_____

_____

Name _____

Part 3: Project-Based Activity

Luke Ridley wants to buy some rawhide bones for Frodo, his dog. He searches online and finds a retailer that sells products for pets. The box sizes (number of rawhides) and prices are shown in the following table.

Box Size	Price
10	$9.90
20	$15.80
50	$34.50
100	$63.00

1. What is the unit price for each box of rawhides? Which size is the best value?

   _____
   _____
   _____
   _____
   _____

2. Luke learns that the rawhide manufacturer offers the rebates shown in the following table. What is the unit price of each box size after the rebate? Which size is the best value?

Box Size	Rebate
10	$0
20	$3.00
50	$10.00
100	$0

   _____
   _____
   _____
   _____
   _____
   _____

3. Luke decides to buy a box of 100 rawhides and some other items. The items he orders are shown in the following table. There are no rebates for any of these items. However, Luke uses a special coupon for first-time customers and gets a 10% discount off all items except the rawhides and dog food. What is the final price of one unit of each item after the discount (but before sales tax)? What is the final price of the entire order including 5% sales tax?

Item	Quantity	Price
Rawhides, box of 100	1	$63.00
High protein dog food, 16 ounce can	24	$2.29
Sweater, size XXXL	2	$19.99
Sausage chew toy	3	$3.49
Dog booties	1	$11.00
Personalized food dish	1	$18.99
Toothbrush	4	$6.99

_____
_____
_____
_____
_____
_____
_____
_____

4. Luke opens a charge account with a $500 credit limit to make the purchase from the previous question. In addition, he makes three purchases later in the month for $111.69, $12.62, and $38.95 including tax. What is Luke's charge account balance at the end of the month? How much more can Luke purchase without exceeding his credit limit?

_____
_____
_____

Name _____

5. Frodo needs obedience training. Luke decides to enroll him in one of two schools: the Good Doggie Training Academy or Carl's Canine Camp. Each school offers a contract. The details are shown in the following table. The $200 early payment discount is available if the entire contract is paid at the time of enrollment. Calculate the total cost of each contract. Assume Luke pays early at Carl's and takes the discount. Which contract is least expensive?

	Good Doggie Training Academy	**Carl's Canine Camp**
Contract length	12 months	12 months
Monthly cost	$80	$100
Lessons per month	2	2
Enrollment fee	$150	$25
Early payment discount	None	$200

_____

_____

_____

Notes

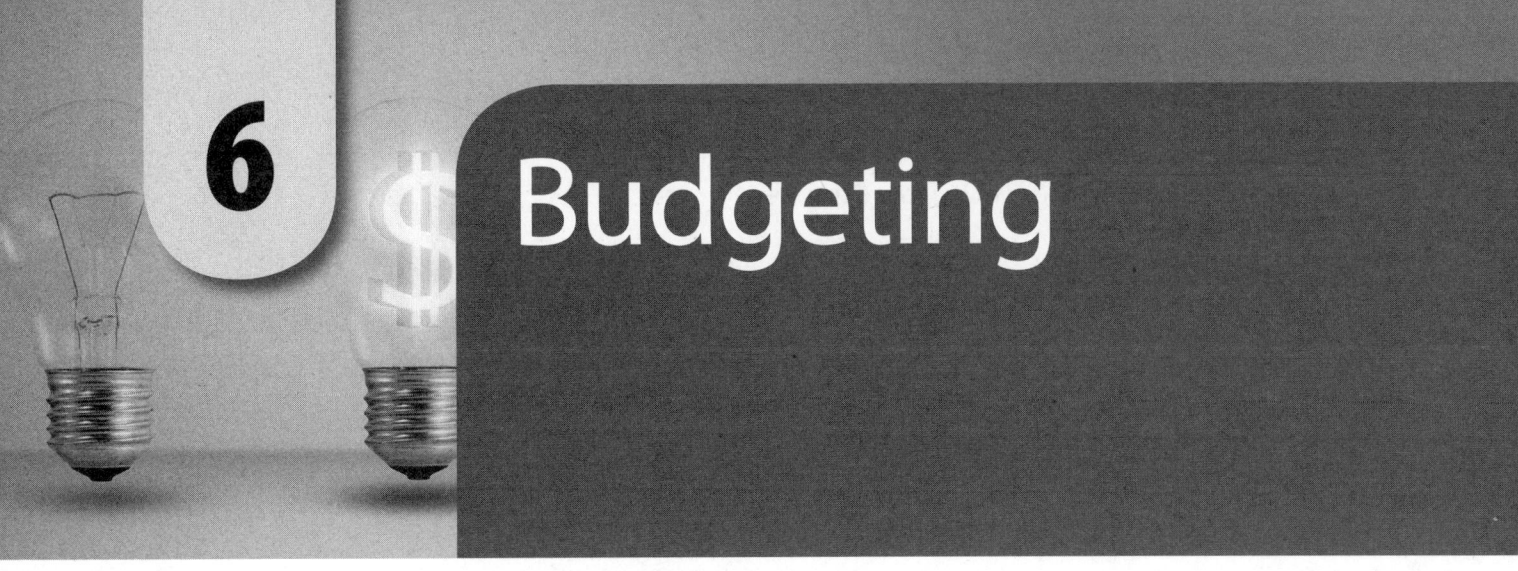

6 Budgeting

Name _____ Date _____ Period _____

Part 1: Chapter Review

Multiple Choice

Choose the letter of the correct answer to each question.

1. _____ A plan for how your income is going to be used and spent is called
   A. a cash flow statement.
   B. a budget.
   C. variable income analysis.
   D. fixed income analysis.

2. _____ People can keep track of their money
   A. by combining households.
   B. with good recordkeeping.
   C. by cutting variable expenses.
   D. with the consumer price index.

3. _____ Examples of recordkeeping include
   A. maintaining check registers.
   B. saving printed receipts.
   C. using personal finance software.
   D. All of the above.

4. _____ Saving money
   A. is an important financial goal.
   B. results in good recordkeeping.
   C. depends mostly on variable income.
   D. All of the above.

5. _____ Which of the following is a fixed expense?
   A. Entertainment
   B. Clothing
   C. Gifts
   D. Rent

6. _____ Which of the following is a variable expense?
   A. Rent
   B. Insurance
   C. Entertainment
   D. Interest income

7. _____ Which of the following is *not* a cash inflow?
   A. Paycheck from a salaried job
   B. Money from sale of stock
   C. Savings
   D. Money received as an inheritance

8. _____ Net cash flow equals
   A. cash inflows minus cash outflows.
   B. fixed income minus fixed expense.
   C. fixed income minus variable expense.
   D. cash inflows plus cash outflows.

9. _____ What is the difference between a cash flow statement and a budget?
   A. There is no difference between the two.
   B. A cash flow statement reports actual activity; a budget is a plan.
   C. Cash flow statements are audited; budgets are not.
   D. A cash flow statement can be adjusted; a budget cannot.

10. _____ Which of the following is an example of a measurable financial goal?
    A. Preparing a budget
    B. Measuring inflation
    C. Measuring cash flow
    D. Getting out of debt

Name _____

Fill in the Blank

Using the terms provided, choose the correct answer for each statement.

- budget
- cash flow statement
- cash inflow
- consumer price index
- fixed expense
- fixed income
- inflation
- net cash flow
- optional expense
- recordkeeping

1. Blaine wants to prepare a(n) _____ so he can plan to control his expenses and save money.

2. Blaine prepared a(n) _____ so he can review where he actually received and spent cash last year.

3. Last year, Blaine received $40,000 cash from wages, $7,000 from the sale of a car, and $2,000 in lottery winnings. Thus, his _____ was $49,000.

4. Blaine monitored last year's expenses by reviewing his checking account register and printed receipts. These are _____ activities.

5. Blaine's cash inflow exceeded his cash outflow last year, meaning his _____ was positive.

6. An increase in the _____ over a period of time indicates there has been a general increase in prices.

7. The purchasing power of cash declines during a period of _____.

8. Blaine spent $1,500 for gas last year. Most of his driving was to work, but approximately 10% of his driving was for weekend fishing trips. As a result, approximately $150 was a(n) _____.

9. Blaine's budgeted income for next year includes $40,000 from his salaried employment. This would be _____.

10. Blaine budgets a $900 monthly expense for rent, which will remain the same for two years under a lease. This would be a(n) _____.

Open Response

Answer each of the questions that follow.

1. Suppose your net cash flow is negative for the current month. Does this necessarily mean you are not handling your finances properly?

2. Suppose you have no debt. Does this necessarily mean you are handling your finances properly?

3. Do you think it is important to consider the impact of inflation when setting measurable financial goals? Why?

4. Suppose you want to save more money. Do you think this goal will be easier to accomplish if you currently spend more on necessities or on optional expenses? Why?

5. What are two expenses that can be shared to result in significant savings when households are combined?

Name _____

Part 2: Chapter Activities

Section 6.1 Creating a Budget

Oscar's goal is to save an average of $150 a month for a down payment on a house, but he is concerned that his savings are falling short of this amount. His financial information for the last three months is shown in the following table.

		July	August	September
Income:	Wages	$2,200	$2,200	$2,200
Expenses:	Rent	$750	$750	$750
	Car lease	$300	$300	$300
	Utilities	$240	$240	$240
	Phone	$75	$75	$75
	Gas	$165	$165	$165
	Food at home	$200	$200	$200
	Food at restaurants	$100	$145	$165
	Entertainment	$175	$250	$275
	Miscellaneous	$25	$75	$100

A. Calculate Oscar's total expenses for each month. Then calculate the monthly mean of these three totals.

_____
_____

B. What amount did Oscar have available to save each month? Assume Oscar saved all the money available for saving in July, August, and September. Is he meeting or falling short of his goal to save an average $150 a month?

_____
_____

C. Oscar thinks he can save money by combining households. He asks his buddy, Norman, if he wants to share an apartment. The monthly rent for the new apartment is $1,100, with utility expenses of $300. Oscar and Norman will split these costs evenly. How much will Oscar save each month by combining households?

_____
_____

D. Suppose Oscar shares an apartment with Norman and keeps all his other expenses and his income at the same level as in September. What amount will he have available to save each month?

_____
_____

Section 6.2 Cash Flow

Cash inflows and cash outflows for five people are shown in the following table.

Description	Ray	Jorge	Faye	Chin	Al
Deposits and additions	$3,000.99	$200.77	$884.79	$4,332.45	$438.09
Checks paid	$1,000.00	$250.88	$233.09	$100.00	$412.67
ATM and debit card withdrawals	$200.00	$60.00	$100.00	$0	$40.00
Electronic withdrawals	$1,239.43	$0	$456.22	$2,900.54	$100.00

A. What are the total cash inflow and the total cash outflow amounts for each person?

___

B. What is the net cash flow for each person?

___

Name _____

Section 6.3 Setting Financial Goals

Kenwin hopes to enroll at Claremore College in four years and looks up the tuition rate. He sees the following:

Today	$20,000
One year ago	$19,048
Four years ago	$16,394

A. What was the inflation rate of tuition at Claremore last year?

_____

B. What was the average annual inflation at Claremore over the last four years?

_____

C. Assume that tuition at Claremore will increase over the next four years at the same annual inflation rate as the last four years. How much money will Kenwin need for his first year of tuition when he enrolls in four years?

_____

Math for Financial Literacy Workbook

Part 3: Project-Based Activity

Bonnie is concerned that her savings account balance declined last year, so she decided to review her finances. Her cash inflows and cash outflows for last year are shown in the following table.

Item	Cash Inflow	Cash Outflow
Wages	$30,500	
Utilities		$3,116
Medical care		$519
Auto payments		$3,588
Insurance		$2,339
Rent		$10,800
Bonus	$1,000	
Sale of motorcycle	$1,000	
Gas		$1,600
Food		$4,260
Gifts		$500
Entertainment		$2,676
Clothing		$1,953
Phone bill		$840
Miscellaneous		$2,206

1. Using the data shown above, what was Bonnie's total cash inflow? What was her total cash outflow? What was her net cash flow?

   _____

   _____

   _____

2. Bonnie wants to save $4,000 annually so she can someday make a down payment on a house. She prepares a budget for next year's income, making the following adjustments:
   - Bonnie was just given a pay raise and expects her wages to increase 3%.
   - She expects next year's bonus to increase $100 over last year.
   - There are no plans to sell anything next year.

   What is Bonnie's budget amount for income for next year?

   _____

Name _____

3. Bonnie expects to make the following adjustments next year that affect expenses:
   - She decides to share a new apartment with her best friend, Giselle. They will evenly split the $1,250 monthly rent and $350 monthly utilities expense.
   - She will reduce food expense by $300 annually by eating more meals at home.
   - Entertainment spending will be reduced by $500 annually.
   - She will spend only $100 a month for miscellaneous expenses and $125 a month for clothes.
   - All other expenses will remain the same as last year.

   What is Bonnie's budget amount for expenses for next year?

   _____

4. Based on Bonnie's budget for income and expenses, how much money can she save next year? Will this meet her $4,000 annual savings goal?

   _____

5. Bonnie wants to save $40,000 for a home down payment. So far she has saved $12,000. How many years will it take to reach her goal if she saves $4,000 a year?

   _____

6. Last year, there was overall inflation in the economy of 2%, as measured by the Consumer Price Index. Do you think the level of inflation might impact her budget for next year? Explain.

   _____

   _____

   _____

Notes

7 Credit Cards

Name _____ Date _____ Period _____

Part 1: Chapter Review

Multiple Choice

Choose the letter of the correct answer to each question.

1. _____ A credit card
   A. allows you to borrow an unlimited amount of money.
   B. is the same as a debit card.
   C. allows you to spend money that is loaned by a financial institution.
   D. is available to anyone who has a savings account at a bank or credit union.

2. _____ A credit card
   A. is a revolving line of credit.
   B. has no credit limits.
   C. has no credit limit if your FICO score remains above 700.
   D. sometimes calculates the interest charge using the grace period method.

3. _____ What is a potential drawback of using a credit card?
   A. No credit limits
   B. No finance charges
   C. Cash back rewards
   D. High finance charges

4. _____ Who would likely get the largest credit limit?
   A. A college student with a part-time job and no student loans
   B. A salaried employee making $100,000 annually with no debt
   C. A salaried employee making $100,000 annually with $500,000 debt
   D. All applicants must be given the same credit limit by law

5. _____ A finance charge is
   A. impossible to avoid when using a credit card.
   B. a fee associated with credit.
   C. a fee associated with debit cards.
   D. limited by law to 15% APR.

6. _____ Which statement is false regarding a credit report?
   A. A credit report is used to calculate your credit score.
   B. A credit report shows how much you owe.
   C. A credit report shows how good you are at making payments on time.
   D. A credit report is the same as a credit score.

7. _____ Credit card companies make money through
   A. finance charges.
   B. annual fees.
   C. late fees.
   D. All of the above.

8. _____ A grace period is a period of time during which you can
   A. pay off your balance and not incur a finance charge.
   B. exceed your credit limit.
   C. get an interest free cash advance.
   D. All of the above.

9. _____ A cash advance on a credit card
   A. usually has no fee.
   B. usually has a grace period.
   C. is a way to get cash from the card's line of credit.
   D. usually cannot be received using an automated teller machine.

10. _____ A FICO score is
   A. the same as a debt-to-income ratio.
   B. the most common credit score.
   C. a tool to compute cash advance fees.
   D. a ratio that is part of the average daily balance method.

Chapter 7 Credit Cards

Name _____

Fill in the Blank

Using the terms provided, choose the correct answer for each statement.

available credit
cash advance
credit card
credit card statement
credit report

FICO score
finance charge
grace period
late fee
line of credit

1. Judy applies to City Bank for a(n) _____ so she can borrow to make purchases every month.

2. The bank runs a(n) _____ on Judy to look at her credit history and assess her ability to incur additional debt.

3. City Bank approves Judy's credit card application after reviewing her credit report and seeing her _____ of 720, indicating that her credit is good.

4. The bank gives Judy a $3,000 _____, which allows her to make purchases on credit and owe money up to that amount.

5. City Bank sends Judy a(n) _____ at the end of the month, which shows she made $1,600 in purchases.

6. Judy's credit limit is $3,000 and her outstanding balance is $1,600, indicating that her _____ is $1,400.

7. Judy will incur no finance charge if she pays all of her $1,600 outstanding balance before the _____ ends.

8. Judy pays only $1,000 of her $1,600 outstanding credit card balance and incurs a(n) _____ as a result.

9. Unfortunately, Judy forgets to make even a minimum required payment on her outstanding balance before the specified due date. As a result, City Bank charges a(n) _____.

10. Judy gets a $500 _____ from her line of credit through an automated teller machine.

Copyright Goodheart-Willcox Co., Inc.
May not be reproduced or posted to a publicly accessible website.

Open Response

Answer each of the questions that follow.

1. Identify two advantages of using a credit card to make purchases instead of cash.

   _____
   _____
   _____
   _____

2. What are three charges or fees you can incur when using a credit card, and how can you avoid them?

   _____
   _____
   _____
   _____

3. Why is it complicated to calculate the interest charge on a credit card?

   _____
   _____
   _____
   _____

4. What are two reasons it is important to promptly open and review your credit card statement when it arrives in the mail?

   _____
   _____
   _____
   _____

5. Give a potential advantage of taking out a debt consolidation loan.

   _____
   _____
   _____
   _____

Name _____

Part 2: Chapter Activities

Section 7.1 Credit Basics

Corky has a bank credit card with a $4,000 credit limit. His balance on February 1 was $1,333.65. The transactions he made during the month are shown in the following table.

Date	Transaction	Amount
February 2	Purchase from Stan's Hardware	$269.21
February 4	Purchase from Bi-Lo Grocery	$79.22
February 6	Purchase from Marty's Party Store	$111.22
February 10	Purchase from Hi-Test Gas	$43.16
February 23	Purchase from Booster Bob's	$507.89
February 28	Refund from Stan's Hardware	$124.78

A. What is Corky's balance after February 28?

_____

B. What is Corky's available credit after February 28?

_____

C. The bank raises Corky's credit limit to $5,600 on March 1. What is his new available credit?

_____

Section 7.2 Finance Charges and Fees

Bart has a credit card with a local bank that carries a 15% annual percentage rate (APR).

A. What is the monthly periodic rate for Bart's credit card?

_____

B. The bank uses the unpaid balance method to compute finance charges. The information shown in the following table is from Bart's last statement. What is the unpaid balance on Bart's account?

Date	Description	Amount
September 1	Previous balance	$3,000
September 11	Payment	$2,000
September 21	New purchases	$1,000

_____

C. Calculate Bart's finance charge on the unpaid balance.

_____

D. What is Bart's new balance?

E. Suppose the bank uses the average daily balance method to compute Bart's finance charge. Bart's average daily balance for September 1 through 30 was $2,000. What will the finance charge be? Which method results in the higher finance charge: the unpaid balance method or the daily balance method?

Section 7.3 Debt Management

The following table shows income and debt information for three people.

Description	Anna	Wayne	Sakura
Annual gross income	$22,800.00	$39,600.00	$60,000.00
Monthly loan payments:			
Mortgage	$0	$645.76	$0
Car loan	$229.00	$319.00	$479.00
Student loan	$0	$149.88	$0
Boat loan	$0	$0	$179.89
Home improvement loan	$120.55	$175.96	$0

A. Calculate the debt-to-income ratio for each person.

B. According to this measure, which person would be in the best position to take on additional debt? Which would be in the worst position?

Chapter 7   Credit Cards   65

Name _____

Part 3: Project-Based Activity

Chandra has a credit card from Great City Bank with a $7,000 credit limit and a 24% APR. The following table shows transactions from Chandra's last statement.

Date	Activity	Amount
April 1	Previous balance	$2,000
April 6	Payment	$1,000
April 11	Purchase	$500
April 16	Purchase	$1,000
April 21	Purchase	$500
April 26	Purchase	$500

1. What is the monthly periodic rate on Chandra's credit card?

   _____

2. Assume the bank uses the unpaid balance method to calculate the finance charge. Determine the following: the unpaid balance, the finance charge, the new balance as of April 30, and the available credit.

   _____

   _____

   _____

   _____

3. Assume the bank changes practices and uses the average daily balance method to calculate the finance charge. What is Chandra's average daily balance for the month?

   _____

4. What is Chandra's finance charge using the average daily balance method?

   _____

5. Chandra gets an offer to transfer her credit card balance to a card at another bank which has a promotional 6% APR for six months. After the first six months, the APR will be 29%. Chandra decides to transfer her balance of $2,000. The bank uses the average daily balance method to calculate the finance charge. Chandra's transactions for June are shown in the following table. What is Chandra's finance charge using the average daily balance method and the promotional APR?

Date	Activity	Amount
June 1	Previous balance	$2,000
June 7	Payment	$1,500
June 13	Purchase	$500
June 16	Purchase	$1,000
June 23	Purchase	$500
June 26	Purchase	$500

6. What would be Chandra's finance charge using the average daily balance method and the regular APR of 29%? Suppose Chandra has a balance and transactions similar to those for June in the following months after the promotional APR has expired. Do you think changing to the new credit card was a good decision?

7. Chandra earns $42,000 annually in gross income. She makes the following monthly loan payments: mortgage, $695.95; auto, $249.00; and credit cards, $300.00. What is her debt-to-income ratio?

8. Chandra wants to buy a new house that will raise her monthly mortgage payment from $695.95 to $925.00. However, she does not want her debt-to-income ratio to exceed 36%. What will be her debt-to-income ratio with the new mortgage payment? Can she afford the new house?

9. Chandra gets a second job that increases her monthly gross income by $600. Now can she afford the new house?

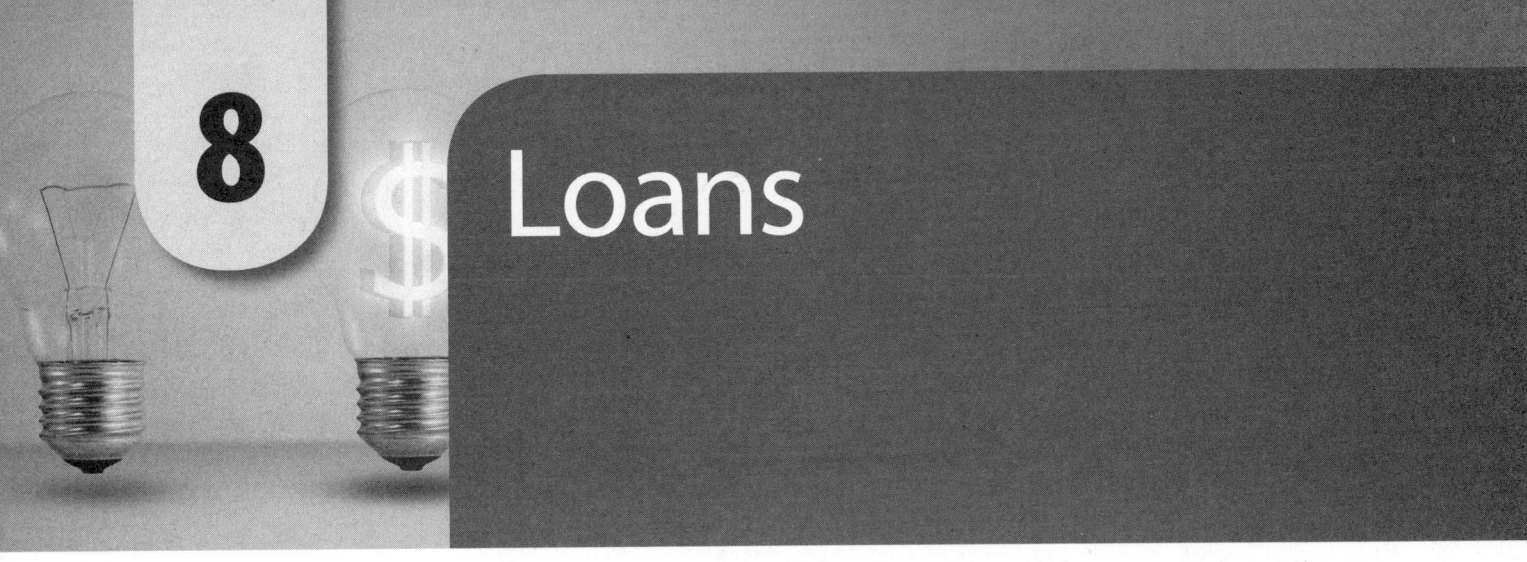

8 Loans

Name _____ Date _____ Period _____

Part 1: Chapter Review

Multiple Choice

Choose the letter of the correct answer to each question.

1. _____ The original sum of money borrowed is called the
   A. principal.
   B. collateral.
   C. lien.
   D. installment.

2. _____ The length of time that money will be borrowed is the
   A. ordinary interest period.
   B. principal period.
   C. amortization period.
   D. term.

3. _____ Something of value that is pledged as security for a loan is called
   A. a lien.
   B. amortized principal.
   C. a promissory note.
   D. collateral.

4. _____ A promissory note specifies
   A. only the interest rate.
   B. only the principal.
   C. the principal, interest rate, and term.
   D. the principal and term, but not the interest rate.

5. _____ A single payment loan
   A. is repaid in one payment with interest.
   B. is repaid in one payment without interest.
   C. must always have a down payment.
   D. must always have collateral.

Copyright Goodheart-Willcox Co., Inc.
May not be reproduced or posted to a publicly accessible website.

67

6. _____ Which method is used to calculate the interest for money borrowed less than a year?
   A. Ordinary interest method
   B. Level payment method
   C. Annual interest amount
   D. Ordinary installment method

7. _____ A down payment
   A. increases the risk to the lender.
   B. is the portion of a purchase which the borrower pays up front.
   C. is the same as an early loan repayment.
   D. must be at least 10%.

8. _____ Pawnshops
   A. can buy personal property but cannot sell it.
   B. offer loans that require collateral.
   C. offer loans that do not require collateral.
   D. are another name for payday lenders.

9. _____ Which of the following is a typical feature of a student loan?
   A. No repayment is required unless the student graduates.
   B. No repayment is required until after the student graduates or stops attending school.
   C. No repayment is required if the student graduates.
   D. No interest is charged after the student graduates.

10. _____ A title loan is
    A. available with or without collateral.
    B. a long-term, low-interest loan.
    C. a short-term, high-interest loan.
    D. another name for pawnshop loan.

Chapter 8 Loans **69**

Name _____

Fill in the Blank

Using the terms provided, choose the correct answer for each statement.

    collateral
    down payment
    early repayment
    installment loan
    lien

    payday loan
    principal
    scholarship
    student loan
    term

1. Rocky buys a $15,000 car but only has enough cash to make a $2,000 _____.

2. After making a $2,000 down payment on his $15,000 car, Rocky borrows the rest to make the purchase. The _____ amount of his loan is $13,000.

3. Rocky will repay his car loan in equal monthly amounts over four years. This is called a(n) _____.

4. Rocky's car loan has a(n) _____ of four years, over which he will make monthly payments until it is paid off.

5. Rocky's loan allows for _____ whereby he can pay down the loan before the end of its term and reduce his interest cost.

6. Rocky's new car will serve as _____ for his loan, meaning the vehicle is pledged as security in case he can't make his car payments.

7. The lending bank places a(n) _____ on Rocky's car, giving it the right to claim the vehicle if necessary to repay the loan.

8. Rocky needs money to help pay his college tuition, so he applies for a(n) _____, which he won't have to repay until after he stops attending school.

9. Rocky's outstanding academic achievements earned him a(n) _____, which covers half of his tuition.

10. A few years ago, Rocky was short of cash and needed $150 quickly for an emergency. He borrowed the money with a(n) _____ and repaid it a week later after he received his next paycheck.

Copyright Goodheart-Willcox Co., Inc.
May not be reproduced or posted to a publicly accessible website.

Open Response

Answer each of the questions that follow.

1. What is the biggest difference between a single-payment loan and an installment loan?

   _____
   _____
   _____
   _____

2. Why do lenders require collateral on some loans?

   _____
   _____
   _____
   _____

3. What three important loan details are specified in a promissory note?

   _____
   _____
   _____
   _____

4. Student loans are attractive because they usually don't have to be repaid until after graduation or when the person stops attending school. Why is this a potential drawback?

   _____
   _____
   _____
   _____

5. What are two extreme consequences of not repaying a loan under the terms of the agreement?

   _____
   _____
   _____
   _____

Name _____

Part 2: Chapter Activities

Section 8.1 Loans and Interest

Anson shops at four different furniture stores and finds that each one sells the identical sofa he wants. He doesn't have enough cash to make a purchase; however, each store offers immediate delivery with one-year financing. This financing requires a single payment due in one year with interest. The following table shows the sofa price at each store along with the annual interest rate.

Store	Sofa Price	Annual Interest Rate
Seating City	$1,099	15.0%
James Furniture	$1,125	11.0%
Sofa Galaxy	$1,209	6.0%
Universe of Sofas	$1,249	3.0%

A. Calculate the total amount Anson will pay in a year at each store. Where should he buy the sofa?

_____

_____

_____

_____

_____

B. Suppose Sofa Galaxy runs a special promotion with one-year financing at a 0% interest rate. How much will Anson pay in a year? Should he buy the sofa at Sofa Galaxy?

_____

_____

C. Suppose Anson has the cash to make an immediate purchase. Where should he buy the sofa? How much less would this cost than the lowest amount paid if he finances the purchase (at the rates shown in question A)?

_____

_____

Section 8.2 Installment Loans

Rita just bought a car for $15,000. She paid 20% down and borrowed the remainder at an annual interest rate of 9.0%. The loan will be repaid over four years with monthly payments of $298.62.

A. How much was Rita's down payment and how much did she borrow?

_____

_____

B. For Rita's first monthly payment, calculate the amount paid for interest and the amount applied to the principal balance.

_____

_____

Section 8.3 High-Interest Loans

Patsy needs a $1,200 loan. She is considering either a title loan on her car or a pawnshop loan on her diamond bracelet.

A. A local finance company offers a $1,200 loan on her car, which is worth $4,750. The fee is 23.0% of the loan amount for a 30-day term. How much will Patsy have to pay after 30 days?

_____

_____

B. A pawnshop offers a $1,200 loan on her bracelet, which is worth $5,900. The term is 30 days, and the interest charge is 1.65% plus a 24% fee for storage and handling. How much will Patsy have to pay after 30 days?

_____

_____

C. Why might Patsy prefer the title loan over the pawnshop loan?

_____

_____

D. Why might Patsy prefer the pawnshop over the title loan?

_____

_____

Name _____

Section 8.4 Student Loans

Tammy is planning to attend college and graduate in four years. The annual cost of tuition and fees is $31,200. Tammy has scholarships, grants, and a work-study program to cover costs of $19,100 a year. The remainder will be paid for with student loans.

A. How much will Tammy need to borrow each year? How much will she need to borrow over four years?

_____

_____

B. Tammy's total student loan balance will be repaid after graduation in monthly installments over 10 years. Her monthly loan payment will be $484. How much interest will she pay when the loans are completely paid off after 10 years?

_____

_____

C. Tammy is told that as a general rule, her monthly student loan payment should not exceed 10% of her expected monthly gross income in her first job after graduation. Tammy expects to earn $36,000 a year as a teacher after she graduates. Will her student loan balance be too high using this rule?

_____

_____

D. Identify two possible strategies to keep Tammy's monthly loan payments from exceeding 10% of her expected gross income.

_____

_____

_____

Part 3: Project-Based Activity

Kerry needs equipment for his new landscaping business and borrows $13,000 from his cousin Norm. He signs the following promissory note:

> The borrower, Kerry Needham, borrows from the lender, Norman Goode, the sum of $13,000 for a period of one year. Mr. Needham will pay an annual interest rate of 11.0% and promises to pay the loan in full, including all interest, at the end of one year.

1. How much interest is due based on the information in the promissory note?

   _____

2. Kerry also borrows $4,300 from a local bank on March 13 to buy fertilizer and herbicides. He repays the loan with interest on October 21 after the landscaping season ends. The annual interest rate is 10.75%. How much interest does Kerry pay? Use the exact interest method.

   _____

3. Kerry's new business does well, so he buys a new truck for $23,512. He makes a down payment and finances the remainder with an $18,000 loan at a 9.75% annual interest rate. The loan is to be repaid in monthly payments of $454.37 over four years. Find the interest amount, the principal amount, and the remaining principal balance at the end of each month for the first four months of the loan repayment.

   _____
   _____
   _____
   _____

4. Suppose Kerry makes the first four payments on his car loan and wants to pay off the entire loan when he makes his fifth payment. What will be the amount of his fifth payment?

   _____

5. Calculate Kerry's total interest if he repays the loan over 48 months. Then calculate his total interest if he pays off the entire loan early with his fifth payment. How much interest does Kerry save by paying off the loan early?

   _____
   _____
   _____

Name _____

6. Kerry needs $2,000 to cover emergency repairs on his equipment. Unfortunately, his savings are depleted because his business is going through a slow period. He decides to borrow the money and expects to repay it in 30 days. The following table shows details on three loans he is considering: a credit card cash advance, a title loan, and a pawnshop loan. Calculate the total interest and fees for each loan. Which one has the lowest cost?

Loan Type	Loan Amount	Interest Rate/Fees	Collateral
Credit card cash advance	$2,000	3.0% fee plus 28.0% APR	None required
Title loan	$2,000	22.0% fee	Business truck valued at $10,000
Pawnshop loan	$2,000	1.5% interest plus 20.0% storage fee	Sports memorabilia valued at $10,000

_____

_____

_____

7. Suppose the credit card cash advance is not available. Kerry must choose between the title and pawnshop loan. Which loan do you think Kerry should choose and why?

_____

_____

Notes

9 Housing

Name _____ Date _____ Period _____

Part 1: Chapter Review

Multiple Choice

Choose the letter of the correct answer to each question.

1. _____ What would be specified in a lease agreement?
   A. Term of lease
   B. Rent amount
   C. Description of the property
   D. All of the above.

2. _____ A security deposit is
   A. a payment made by the renter that is held to cover damage.
   B. the first and last month's rent paid by the lessee in advance.
   C. another name for a down payment on a mortgage.
   D. the deductible amount of an insurance policy.

3. _____ A replacement cost insurance policy will pay
   A. what it actually costs to replace an item.
   B. the replacement cost or actual cash value, whichever is less.
   C. what it actually costs to replace an item, excluding inflation.
   D. the replacement cost if there is at least a $1,000 deductible.

4. _____ Renters insurance covers the
   A. rent payment.
   B. renter's dwelling.
   C. renter's belongings.
   D. deductible portion of replacement cost.

5. _____ A loan made for the purpose of purchasing a home is a(n)
   A. title loan.
   B. mortgage.
   C. amortization loan.
   D. full amortization loan.

6. _____ The process of paying down a loan through regular payments of principal and interest is called
   A. equity financing.
   B. refinancing.
   C. a balloon payment.
   D. amortization.

7. _____ The part of a loss for which the holder of an insurance policy is responsible is called the
   A. deductible.
   B. security deposit.
   C. amortized value.
   D. replacement cost.

8. _____ Refinancing is
   A. the process of making a balloon payment.
   B. replacing one insurance provider with another.
   C. replacing one mortgage with another that has a lower interest rate.
   D. changing an insurance policy from actual cash value to replacement value.

9. _____ What is a factor that determines the property tax on a home?
   A. Actual cash value
   B. Assessed value
   C. Replacement value
   D. Insurance value

10. _____ The amount that the value of a home exceeds what is owed on the home is called the
    A. equity.
    B. remaining mortgage balance.
    C. assessed value.
    D. balloon payment residual.

Name _____

Fill in the Blank

Using the terms provided, choose the correct answer for each statement.

- amortization
- appraisal
- closing costs
- deductible
- lease
- mortgage loan
- property tax
- renters insurance
- replacement cost policy
- security deposit

1. Nina signs a(n) _____ for her new apartment for a one-year term at $800 a month rent.

2. Before moving into her new apartment, Nina pays a $1,200 _____ to the owner of the property, who holds the money to cover any damages.

3. Nina buys _____ to cover her belongings in the event they are stolen or damaged in a fire or some other disaster.

4. Nina buys a(n) _____ from her insurance company, which will pay what it actually costs to replace any items covered in a claim.

5. Nina's insurance policy carries a $500 _____, meaning she must pay $500 of any insured loss.

6. Nina's friend Inga buys a house for $90,000, for which she makes a $20,000 down payment and finances the remaining $70,000 with a(n) _____.

7. The mortgage lender wants a(n) _____ of the value of Inga's house to ensure it will be adequate collateral for the loan.

8. Inga pays _____ when she buys her house, including fees for legal work, document filing, loan application, and an appraisal.

9. After buying her house, Inga pays _____, which is levied by the city each year to fund local activities, such as those of the local school district.

10. Inga will repay her mortgage by making monthly payments of interest and principal calculated through a process called _____.

Open Response

Answer each of the questions that follow.

1. An apartment is available for rent at $800 a month with either a two-year lease or a month-to-month agreement. Suppose you think rental rates will be soon be going up. Would you want the two-year lease? Explain.

   _____
   _____
   _____
   _____

2. What is the difference between what is covered by a homeowners insurance policy and a renters insurance policy? Which do you think would be more expensive?

   _____
   _____
   _____
   _____

3. Why do policies with higher deductibles cost less than ones with lower deductibles?

   _____
   _____
   _____
   _____

4. Homeowners usually refinance their mortgages when interest rates are falling rather than increasing. Why?

   _____
   _____
   _____
   _____

5. When budgeting for the cost of owning a home, why are property taxes just as important to consider as the mortgage payment?

   _____
   _____
   _____
   _____

Name _____

Part 2: Chapter Activities

Section 9.1 Renting

Millie wants to buy a renters insurance policy. Her insurance agent gives her two choices: a replacement cost policy for $289 annually or an actual cash value policy for $199 annually.

A. What is the monthly bill for each policy, including a $1.50 monthly partial payment fee?

_____
_____

B. Millie needs the insurance mainly to get new furniture and clothes in the event that a fire or other disaster damages her property. The replacement cost of these items would be about $7,000, while the actual cash value is only $1,000. Which policy should she buy?

_____
_____

C. Suppose Millie needs the insurance mainly to cover some expensive jewelry, which might be stolen if there is a burglary. The jewelry's replacement cost and actual cash value are identical. Which policy should she buy?

_____
_____

Section 9.2 Purchasing a Home

Randy wants to buy a house priced at $128,900. The lender wants a down payment of at least 20%.

A. Determine the amount of a 20% down payment and the amount Randy will need to finance with a mortgage.

B. Randy did not consider closing costs when planning his home purchase. A real estate agent tells him to budget for the costs shown in the following table. What is the total of the closing fees that Randy should expect to pay at closing?

Closing Fees	Estimated Amount
Legal	$600
Document filing	$225
Loan application	$800
Appraisal	$300
Inspection	$175
Title insurance	$835

C. How much money will Randy need to cover his down payment and closing fees?

D. Randy just bought a house with annual bills of $3,912.87 for property taxes and $912.50 for homeowners insurance. His mortgage lender requires that he make monthly payments for taxes and insurance into an escrow account. What will be Randy's monthly escrow payment?

Name _____

Section 9.3 Mortgage Payments

Tiffany buys a house for $93,750. She makes a 20% down payment and finances the remaining amount with a 30-year mortgage at a 7% APR.

A. How much is Tiffany's down payment and mortgage?

_____

_____

B. Calculate Tiffany's monthly payment using the following table.

Monthly Payment Per $1,000 of Loan Amortization

Interest Rate	15 Years	20 Years	30 Years
5.5%	$8.18	$6.88	$5.68
6.0%	$8.44	$7.17	$6.00
6.5%	$8.72	$7.46	$6.32
7.0%	$8.99	$7.76	$6.66
7.5%	$9.28	$8.06	$7.00

_____

_____

C. Calculate the amount of the first monthly payment that is for interest, the amount applied to principal, and the new loan balance.

_____

_____

D. After 15 years, her mortgage balance declined to $53,343.66. Tiffany can refinance this balance for the remaining 15 years at 5.5%. What will be her new monthly payment? How much interest will Tiffany save over the remaining 15 years of her mortgage after refinancing?

_____

_____

Part 3: Project-Based Activity

Marsha needs a place to live and wants to either rent an apartment or buy a house. She is on a budget and doesn't want her monthly housing expense to exceed $850. Her housing expense as a renter would include rent and insurance. As a homeowner, her housing expense would include a monthly mortgage payment, insurance, and property tax. Marsha finds apartments available at the following locations:

Monthly Rents

Location	One Bedroom	Two Bedrooms
Spring Breeze Apartments	$750	$950
Summer Wind Apartments	$700	$900
Autumn Air Apartments	$875	$1,200

1. Which locations can Marsha consider renting with her budget?

2. What apartments can Marsha consider if she lives with a roommate and splits the rent evenly?

3. Marsha wants a two-bedroom apartment, but she doesn't want a roommate. She might be in luck. All three apartment complexes are running a special promotion: sign a one-year lease and get the first month free. How much will the average monthly rent be on a two-bedroom apartment for a year at each location? Will any of these fit Marsha's budget?

4. Marsha wants renters insurance mainly to cover her clothes and furniture in the event of a fire or other disaster. She estimates it would cost about $8,000 to replace these items. The actual cash value is about $2,000. Her insurance agent offers her two policies. The first is an actual cash value policy at $169 a year. The second is a replacement cost policy at $219 a year. Both have the same $500 deductible. Calculate the monthly insurance bill for each policy, including a $1.50 monthly partial payment fee. Which policy would you recommend she buy?

Name _____

5. Marsha likes the two-bedroom apartment at Summer Wind. Can Marsha get this apartment and a replacement cost insurance policy and stay within her monthly housing budget? (The special rent promotion from question #3 is still available.)

_____

_____

6. Marsha considers buying a house and finds one she likes priced at $80,900. She has $19,350 saved for a down payment and closing costs. The mortgage lender requires a down payment of at least 20%. The following table shows the estimated closing costs. How much cash will Marsha need to cover a 20% down payment and her estimated closing costs? Does she have enough money?

Item	Amount
Legal fees	$535
Document filing fees	$300
Loan application fees	$500
Appraisal fees	$300
Inspection fees	$165
Title insurance	$450

_____

_____

7. If Marsha buys the house with a 20% down payment and borrows the remainder, how much will Marsha borrow?

_____

8. The house Marsha wants to buy is in Pittsburgh, Pennsylvania, and it is assessed at $69,400 for tax purposes. Calculate the annual property tax owed to each jurisdiction and the total tax due. Also calculate her monthly total tax. Pennsylvania defines tax rates using millage.

Taxing Jurisdiction	Tax Rate (‰)
Pittsburgh School District	13.92
Allegheny County	4.69
Allegheny County Community College District	9.17
City of Pittsburgh	10.80

_____

_____

_____

_____

_____

9. Marsha's homeowners insurance would cost $744.32 annually. Calculate her monthly insurance bill. Include a $1.25 monthly partial payment fee.

10. Marsha's monthly mortgage payment is $409.03. Calculate Marsha's total monthly cost of owning a home (including the mortgage payment, property tax, and insurance). Is this amount within her monthly housing budget of $850?

10 Automobiles

Name _____ Date _____ Period _____

Part 1: Chapter Review

Multiple Choice

Choose the letter of the correct answer to each question.

1. _____ The sticker price of a new car is
   A. set by the dealer.
   B. the minimum price set by the manufacturer.
   C. not subject to negotiation.
   D. only a suggested price.

2. _____ A trade-in-allowance is
   A. not available if the selling price is less than the sticker price.
   B. not available if there is a rebate.
   C. a discount resulting from trading in one car for another.
   D. added to the sale price.

3. _____ An auto loan
   A. is available for terms of 3, 4, 5, and 15 years.
   B. is an installment loan which is paid monthly.
   C. usually requires no collateral.
   D. can only be offered for a car sold at sticker price.

4. _____ The loss of an asset's value over time is called
   A. amortization.
   B. equalization.
   C. depreciation.
   D. normalization.

5. _____ The cost of owning a car includes
   A. gas.
   B. repairs.
   C. insurance.
   D. All of the above.

6. _____ A manufacturer's warranty on a car covers
   A. specific repairs for a specific amount of time or number of miles.
   B. specific repairs for as long as you own the car.
   C. all the maintenance costs for a specific number of miles.
   D. collision repairs but no other repairs.

7. _____ An extended car warranty
   A. eliminates the cost of owning a car.
   B. increases the annual depreciation.
   C. picks up where the manufacturer's warranty leaves off.
   D. All of the above.

8. _____ Which of the following is not a type of coverage in an auto insurance policy?
   A. Liability
   B. Collision
   C. Comprehensive
   D. Extended warranty

9. _____ When a car is totaled, it
   A. can no longer be driven.
   B. has no remaining residual value.
   C. has reached the end of its depreciated life.
   D. has damage which equals or exceeds its value.

10. _____ Which of the following is an attractive feature of auto leasing?
    A. The monthly payment is often lower than for purchasing an auto.
    B. An extended warranty is included.
    C. The lease usually comes with unlimited miles.
    D. The lessee drives the car during the period of lowest depreciation.

Chapter 10 Automobiles

Name _____

Fill in the Blank

Using the terms provided, choose the correct answer for each statement.

auto insurance
automobile dealer
collision coverage
comprehensive coverage
depreciate

extended warranty
liability coverage
MSRP
trade-in allowance
uninsured motorist coverage

1. Celine wants to buy a new car and visits a(n) _____, which sells new and used vehicles.

2. Celine test drives a new car with a(n) _____ of $20,000. She wants to buy it and tries to negotiate a discount with the dealer.

3. The auto dealer and Celine agree on a $19,000 price for the new car. The final price is $14,000 after Celine accepts a $5,000 _____ on the car she is currently driving.

4. Celine's new car comes with a five year/60,000 mile manufacturer's warranty. The dealer offers to sell her a(n) _____, which would cover the car for seven years/100,000 miles.

5. Before Celine can drive her new car, she needs to purchase _____ to cover damage and injuries from auto accidents.

6. Celine's auto insurance includes _____, which pays for damage to her car if she is in an accident.

7. State law requires that Celine carry _____ to pay for property damage or injury to others that is her fault.

8. When Celine is in an accident where the driver of the other car is at fault and has no liability insurance, she is protected by _____.

9. Insurance which protects Celine's car from a wide range of hazards, such as theft, storm damage, and vandalism, is _____.

10. Celine's new car will _____ over time, meaning it will lose value as it gets older.

Open Response

Answer each of the questions that follow.

1. Identify the factors that determine the total price you pay for a new car.

2. The term of a car loan is usually 3, 4, or 5 years. Why not 15 or 30 years like a home mortgage?

3. The straight-line method is the simplest way to calculate the depreciation on a car, but not the most accurate. Why?

4. Why do states require that car owners carry liability coverage?

5. What are some reasons for leasing a car instead of purchasing?

Name _____

Part 2: Chapter Activities

Section 10.1 Owning or Leasing a Car

Lyle wants to buy a new car which has a $27,890 MSRP and a $2,500 manufacturer's rebate. He visits four different dealers and negotiates the best sale price for this car, as well as a trade-in allowance. The results of his negotiations are shown in the following table.

Sale Factor	Dealer #1	Dealer #2	Dealer #3	Dealer #4
MSRP	$27,890	$27,890	$27,890	$27,890
Discount off MSRP	4.0%	$1,000	No discount	$1,200
Trade-in allowance	$10,000	$10,300	$11,200	$9,400

A. Calculate the price of the car at each dealer after trade-in and rebate.

_____
_____
_____
_____

B. Lyle must pay a 4% sales tax, $128 title fee, and $213 license fee. What is the total price of the car at each dealer including TT&L? Where should he buy the car?

_____
_____
_____
_____

C. Now that Lyle has a new car, he decides to sell another older car that he owns. He bought the car for $14,500 and sold it for $4,600. Lyle owned the car for six years. Calculate the amount of depreciation, the average annual depreciation, and the average annual depreciation rate for the car.

_____
_____
_____
_____

Section 10.2 Cost of Owning a Car

Dana bought a new car for $25,400 and wants to estimate the cost of driving 12,000 miles a year. Her car gets 30 miles per gallon and needs the oil changed every 4,000 miles. Gas is $3.35 a gallon and an oil change is $30.00. In addition, the following are the annual premiums from her new insurance policy.

Coverage Type	Annual Premium
Liability (bodily injury)	$74
Liability (property damage)	$4
Collision ($250 deductible)	$279
Comprehensive ($100 deductible)	$89
Uninsured motorist (bodily injury)	$112
Uninsured motorist (property damage)	$73
Road service/car rental	$29

A. What is Dana's annual cost for gas, oil, and insurance, assuming she drives 12,000 miles per year?

B. Dana plans to keep her car five years and expects the resale value to be $10,000 at end of this period. What is the estimated average annual depreciation on her car?

C. What is Dana's annual cost of driving the car including gas, oil, insurance, and average annual depreciation?

Name _____

Part 3: Project-Based Activity

Orson needs a new car and identifies three different models that he likes equally. He then visits car dealers and negotiates the best sales price for each model, along with a trade-in allowance. The following table shows the pricing information for each model.

Sale Factor	Model #1	Model #2	Model #3
MSRP	$25,900	$26,800	$25,500
Discount off MSRP	$1,000	5%	No discount
Manufacturer's rebate	$500	$1,000	None
Trade-in allowance	$3,000	$3,700	$2,800

1. Calculate the price of each car after trade-in and rebate.

   _____
   _____
   _____

2. Orson must pay a 5.0% sales tax, $130 title fee, and $155 license fee for each of the three cars. Determine the total price of each car including TT&L. Which is least expensive?

   _____
   _____
   _____

3. The miles per gallon of gas and miles per oil change for each car model are shown in the following table. Calculate the annual cost of gas and oil changes for each car. Assume gas is $3.50 a gallon and oil changes are $30.00. Orson drives 12,000 miles a year.

Mileage Factor	Model #1	Model #2	Model #3
Miles per gallon	30	25	35
Miles per oil change	4,000	3,000	3,000

   _____
   _____
   _____

4. Orson plans to keep his new car for four years and either resell it or trade it in. He does research on car prices. Estimates for the resale prices for each model are shown in the following table. For each model, calculate the total depreciation, the average annual depreciation, and the average annual depreciation rate. Use the total prices including TT&L (from question #2) as the purchase price in your depreciation calculations.

Estimated Resale Prices

Model #1	Model #2	Model #3
$12,500	$13,000	$13,500

_____

_____

_____

_____

5. Orson calls his insurance agent and gets auto insurance quotes. The annual insurance premium for Model #1 is $800; Model #2, $825; and Model #3, $875. Complete the following table, which lists the various annual costs of driving each model. Then calculate the total amount for each model. Which model is least expensive to drive? (Orson doesn't budget for repairs because each car is covered under a manufacturer's warranty.)

Annual Cost Of Driving

	Model #1	Model #2	Model #3
Gas			
Oil changes			
Average annual depreciation			
Insurance			
Total			

_____

_____

Building Wealth

Name _____ Date _____ Period _____

Part 1: Chapter Review

Multiple Choice

Choose the letter of the correct answer to each question.

1. _____ Wealth is commonly measured by
   A. net worth.
   B. net worth minus liabilities.
   C. net worth plus liabilities.
   D. total assets.

2. _____ Passive income is received from
   A. work.
   B. work and investment income.
   C. investments.
   D. active income after debt reduction.

3. _____ An investment can
   A. earn income.
   B. increase in value over time.
   C. decline in value over time.
   D. All of the above.

4. _____ Bankruptcy
   A. cannot be avoided if your net worth is negative.
   B. can be avoided if you sell all your assets.
   C. occurs when you cannot pay debts when they are due.
   D. All of the above.

5. _____ A bond pays
   A. dividends.
   B. interest.
   C. premiums.
   D. active income.

6. _____ A bond can be priced
   A. only at par value.
   B. only at par value or a discount.
   C. only at par value or a premium.
   D. at par value, a discount, or a premium.

7. _____ Stock dividends are
   A. paid by every company.
   B. paid by every company, but only if the company earns a profit.
   C. not paid by every company.
   D. determined directly by shareholder vote.

8. _____ Spreading money around in multiple investments is known as
   A. passive investment.
   B. diversification.
   C. active investment.
   D. an initial public offering.

9. _____ Mutual funds
   A. have managers who make decisions to buy and sell stocks.
   B. require a minimum $100,000 investment.
   C. offer very little or no diversification.
   D. cannot specialize in certain kinds of stocks.

10. _____ Which is an advantage of investing in a mutual fund?
    A. No taxes
    B. No risk
    C. No fees
    D. Diversification

Name _____

Fill in the Blank

Using the terms provided, choose the correct answer for each statement.

- bonds
- coupon rate
- discount
- diversification
- dividends
- mutual fund
- net worth
- passive income
- stocks
- wealth

1. Rhonda has a financial goal to build _____ so she can afford to travel, support her favorite charities, and retire comfortably.

2. Rhonda has $125,000 in total assets, $50,000 in total liabilities, and a(n) _____ of $75,000.

3. Rhonda earns $45,000 a year, of which $40,000 is from wages. The remaining $5,000 is _____ from interest and dividends on investments.

4. Rhonda invests some of her savings in _____, which are issued by corporations and government entities and pay interest.

5. Rhonda owns a bond with a $1,000 face value and a 6% _____, meaning it pays $60 interest every year.

6. Rhonda purchases a bond for $965, which is a(n) _____ to its $1,000 face value.

7. Rhonda invests part of her savings in _____, which represent ownership in companies.

8. Rhonda collects _____ from her stocks, which are distributions of profits from the companies in which she owns stock.

9. Rhonda does not want to risk having all her savings invested in a single bond or stock, so she spreads her savings into multiple investments. This strategy is called _____.

10. Rhonda purchased shares in a(n) _____, where the money from many investors is combined to buy a diversified group of stocks.

Open Response

Answer each of the questions that follow.

1. What is the difference between active and passive income?

   _____
   _____
   _____
   _____

2. An investment is a purchase you make in hopes of making money. What are two ways an investment can make money?

   _____
   _____
   _____
   _____

3. Gold does not pay interest or dividends or generate any cash income. Can it be considered an investment? Explain.

   _____
   _____
   _____
   _____

4. A bond can make money for investors only through interest income. Do you agree with this statement? Explain.

   _____
   _____
   _____
   _____

5. Identify two reasons why a company might not pay a dividend.

   _____
   _____
   _____
   _____

Name _____

Part 2: Chapter Activities

Section 11.1 What Is Wealth?

The assets and liabilities of five individuals are shown in the following table.

	Maury	Juan	Lori	Fatima	Sid
Assets:					
Checking account	$20,000	$25,000	$25,000	$5,000	$2,000
Savings account	$90,000	$10,000	$40,000	$0	$0
Car	$15,000	$5,000	$20,000	$40,000	$58,000
Home	$100,000	$50,000	$50,000	$100,000	$270,000
Retirement savings	$75,000	$10,000	$15,000	$5,000	$0
Liabilities:					
Credit card debt	$0	$0	$5,000	$5,000	$20,000
Car loan	$0	$0	$15,000	$15,000	$50,000
Mortgage	$0	$0	$30,000	$30,000	$230,000

A. What is the net worth of each person?

_____
_____
_____

B. Who has the most assets, drives the most expensive car, and lives in the most expensive house? Is he or she the wealthiest? Explain.

_____
_____

C. Who has the greatest net worth: Juan, Lori, or Fatima? Who do you think would have the most financial difficulty if she or he suffered a job loss for a year?

_____
_____
_____

D. Suppose Lori pays her car loan and credit card bill down to zero with money from her savings account. What will happen to her net worth?

_____
_____

Section 11.2 Bonds

Byron buys a bond with a $1,000 par value that is quoted at 96.75. It has a 5.0% coupon rate, six years to maturity, and pays interest semiannually.

A. What is the price of the bond?

B. How much annual income will Byron receive from the bond? How much is the amount of each interest payment?

C. How much total interest will he receive if he holds the bond for six years?

D. What is the yield on his bond?

Section 11.3 Stocks and Mutual Funds

Lynn buys 300 shares of XM Company stock at $38.25 a share. The commission on the trade is $7. The stock pays an annual dividend of $1.04 a share.

A. What is the cost of the stocks plus the commission on the trade?

B. How much dividend income will Lynn receive each year?

C. What is the dividend yield on XM Company stock?

D. Lynn is also considering investing in the Riviera Growth Mutual Fund. Information about the fund from last year is shown in the following table. What is the net asset value (NAV) of the fund on January 1 and December 31?

Date	Assets	Liabilities	Number of Shares
January 1	$237,000,000	$1,200,000	21,900,000
December 31	$280,000,000	$1,300,000	23,300,000

Name _____

Part 3: Project-Based Activity

Kattie has been working six years as a physical therapist. Each year she saves some of her earnings, and she deposits the money in her checking and retirement savings accounts. A list of her assets and liabilities are shown in the following table.

Assets		Liabilities	
Checking account	$40,000	Credit card debt	$1,000
Car	$3,000	Car loan	$0
Retirement savings	$10,000	Student loan	$2,000

1. What is Kattie's net worth?
   _____

2. Kattie considers buying a new car for $38,000. She would pay for it with $35,000 from her checking account and a $3,000 trade-in on the car she is now driving. What would be her net worth if she buys the car?
   _____

3. Kattie also considers buying a less expensive car for $13,000. She would pay for it with $10,000 from her checking account and a $3,000 trade-in on the car she is now driving. What would be her net worth if she buys the car?
   _____

4. Kattie buys the $13,000 car. She then decides to invest $25,000 from her checking account in bonds to earn passive income. She buys five each of five different bonds. Each bond has a $1,000 par value. For each bond purchase, calculate the total amount paid for the five bonds, the annual interest received for the five bonds, and the bond yield.

Bond	Number Purchased	Price Quote	Coupon Rate
Bond A	5	$105.00	5.25%
Bond B	5	$102.00	5.50%
Bond C	5	$95.00	4.25%
Bond D	5	$98.00	4.50%
Bond E	5	$100.00	5.00%

_____
_____
_____
_____
_____
_____

5. What is the total amount paid for all the bonds? What is the total annual interest Kattie will receive from all the bonds? What is the yield on Kattie's total investment in the bonds? (Divide the total annual interest by the total amount paid for all the bonds.)

_____

_____

_____

6. How did Kattie's decision to buy a less expensive car ($13,000 versus $38,000) help her build wealth?

_____

_____

_____

7. Kattie invested only in bonds. What are some other types of investments Kattie might have chosen in addition to bonds to have a diversified group of investments?

_____

_____

_____

12 Insurance

Name _____ Date _____ Period _____

Part 1: Chapter Review

Multiple Choice

Choose the letter of the correct answer to each question.

1. _____ Insurance
   A. is a way to share risk.
   B. requires participation by a large group of people.
   C. provides protection from financial loss.
   D. All of the above.

2. _____ The most basic life insurance is
   A. universal life.
   B. term life.
   C. whole term.
   D. whole life.

3. _____ The person who is paid by a life insurance company when the insured dies is the
   A. insured.
   B. coinsured.
   C. beneficiary.
   D. whole life payee.

4. _____ Whole life insurance differs from term life because it
   A. is more expensive.
   B. is permanent.
   C. builds up a cash value.
   D. All of the above.

5. _____ Health insurance provided by an employer is called
   A. coinsurance.
   B. term health insurance.
   C. group health insurance.
   D. universal health insurance.

6. _____ The amount you pay for a doctor visit when you have health insurance is the
   A. copayment.
   B. deductible.
   C. premium.
   D. out-of-pocket premium.

7. _____ What type of insurance replaces income when you cannot work due to illness or injury?
   A. Liability
   B. Disability
   C. Universal
   D. Umbrella

8. _____ An umbrella policy
   A. increases your total amount of liability coverage.
   B. covers storm and flood damage.
   C. eliminates the need for liability insurance.
   D. is another name for group health insurance.

9. _____ To help prevent identity theft
   A. shred important financial documents before discarding them.
   B. immediately report missing credit cards.
   C. be cautious about entering personal information on websites.
   D. All of the above.

10. _____ Travel insurance covers
    A. trip cancellation expenses.
    B. airport parking fees.
    C. bad hotel service.
    D. All of the above.

Name _____

Fill in the Blank

Using the terms provided, choose the correct answer for each statement.

 beneficiary
 cash value
 coinsurance
 copayment
 disability insurance
 group health
 professional liability
 term life
 umbrella policy
 whole life

1. Tom buys a $300,000 life insurance policy. He names his wife as the _____, who will receive the money if he dies.

   _____

2. Tom chooses a simple _____ policy, which will be active for 20 years and guarantee that his premiums will the stay the same over this period.

   _____

3. Tom considered buying a(n) _____ policy, which is a type of permanent life insurance that would be in force until he dies.

   _____

4. Part of the premium for a whole life policy is invested and builds up a(n) _____, which the insured receives if he or she cancels the policy.

   _____

5. Tom receives _____ coverage, which is health insurance provided by his employer.

   _____

6. Tom's health insurance requires that he make a $20 _____ for each doctor visit.

   _____

7. Tom's health insurance requires that he pay 15% of his medical expenses after he meets his deductible, with a maximum out-of-pocket expense of $2,000. This expense sharing arrangement is called _____.

   _____

8. Tom buys _____, which will pay 60% of his salary if he can't work due to illness or injury.

   _____

9. Tom buys a(n) _____ from the insurance company that covers his home and car. This policy increases his liability coverage to $2,000,000.

   _____

10. Tom, who is a teacher, bought _____ insurance to cover issues that may arise related to the quality of his work.

    _____

Open Response

Answer each of the questions that follow.

1. Briefly explain one advantage of term life insurance compared to whole life.

   _____
   _____
   _____
   _____

2. Stacy is married, has three young children, and does not work outside the home. Can you think of a reason she should have life insurance? Explain.

   _____
   _____
   _____
   _____

3. What are three types of out-of-pocket expenses you can incur with health insurance?

   _____
   _____
   _____
   _____

4. What do you share with an insurance company when you have coinsurance?

   _____
   _____
   _____
   _____

5. Samantha, an accountant, is 29 years old and earns $41,000 a year. She is single and has no dependents. Which type of insurance do you think she needs more, life insurance or disability insurance? Briefly explain.

   _____
   _____
   _____
   _____

Name _____

Part 2: Chapter Activities

Section 12.1 Life Insurance

Josh wants to buy a $500,000 term life insurance policy. He goes to the website of an insurance company and finds the monthly premiums for a 10-year and 20-year policy for a man his age in good health. Premiums for both a smoker and a nonsmoker are shown in the following table.

Monthly Premiums

Age 36, good health:	10-Year Term	20-Year Term
Nonsmoker	$18	$30
Smoker	$57	$81

A. Calculate the total premiums of a 10-year and 20-year policy for both a smoker and nonsmoker.

_____

_____

_____

B. Why do you think the premium for a smoker is higher than for a nonsmoker?

_____

_____

C. Why do you think the monthly premiums are higher for a 20-year policy than a 10-year policy?

_____

_____

_____

_____

_____

D. Josh wants enough term life insurance to provide the following financial support for his family:
- Pay off the $56,000 mortgage balance on the family home.
- Set aside $50,000 for each of his two children for college.
- Provide 10 years of his net pay, which is $3,000 a month.

How much insurance should Josh purchase?

_____

_____

E. Three years later, Josh re-evaluates his life insurance needs. He notes the following:
- The family has a new home with a mortgage of $122,000.
- He now has three children, and college costs have been rising. He wants to set aside $75,000 for each child's college fund.
- He still wants to provide 10 years of his net pay, which is now $3,500 a month.

How much insurance should Josh now have?

Section 12.2 Health and Disability Insurance

While it is possible to purchase health insurance as an individual, many people purchase health insurance through a plan offered by an employer. Some employers pay for part of the health insurance premiums for employees.

A. Carol's employer pays half of her $429 monthly health insurance premium. How much does she pay each year for her health insurance?

B. Carol gets married and adds her husband to her health insurance plan at $429 a month. What will be the annual insurance cost for both?

C. Carol's husband begins working for a new employer who offers him health insurance. He will pay half of the $582 monthly premium, and his employer will pay half. How much does he save each year compared to his premiums with Carol's health insurance plan?

D. Carol's policy has a $100 deductible. The insurance company pays 80% of covered medical bills after the deductible has been paid. Carol's maximum out-of-pocket expense is $1,000. Last year, Carol had covered medical bills of $2,179. What amount did Carol have to pay for out-of-pocket expenses?

E. Carol is a 38-year-old lab technician earning $54,000 a year. She has a long-term disability policy which pays 60% of her monthly salary if she cannot work due to illness or injury. What will be the monthly benefit if Carol is disabled?

Name _____

Section 12.3 Other Types of Insurance

Kris wants to buy a round-trip airline ticket from Detroit to Orlando. She searches a travel website and finds two offers for the same flight. The Web Only Super Save offer price is $490. The fare is not refundable for any reason. The second offer is for a Flexible Flyer fare. The price is $683, and it is fully refundable at any time. Kris knows there is a good chance she will have to cancel the trip. She doesn't want to buy the Super Saver ticket because it is not refundable. She prefers not to risk losing $490. She also thinks the fully refundable ticket is too expensive. Kris considers another option: buy the Super Saver ticket and purchase travel insurance, which is 10% of the ticket price. The insurance will cover the cost of her ticket if she cancels.

A. How much will Kris pay in total if she buys the Super Saver ticket and insurance and does not cancel the trip?

_____

B. How much will Kris pay in total if she buys the Super Saver ticket and insurance and does cancel? How much does Kris save by having insurance if she cancels?

_____

C. Kris is a software consultant and carries professional liability insurance. The policy has a $744 annual premium. She gets a 3% discount for paying her monthly premium directly from her checking account. How much is her monthly premium?

_____

Part 3: Project-Based Activity

Seth is a 32-year-old auto technician who just got married, bought a house, and now wants to purchase life insurance.

1. Seth wants enough insurance so his wife can pay off the mortgage and have money equal to five years of his net earnings if he dies. His net pay is $2,550 a month, and the mortgage is $97,000. How much insurance does Seth need?

   _____

2. Suppose Seth and his wife have two children. In addition to paying off the mortgage, he wants enough insurance to provide 15 years of his net pay and $100,000 for college costs for his children. How much insurance does he need?

   _____

3. Seth searches a website which provides life insurance quotes. He finds the monthly premiums for a $250,000 term life policy for a man his age in good health. The premiums shown are for 10-year and 20-year terms, for both a smoker and nonsmoker. Calculate the total cost of premiums for a 10-year and 20-year policy for both a smoker and nonsmoker. How much will Seth save on a 20-year policy if he doesn't smoke?

   Monthly Premiums

Age 32, good health:	10-Year Term	20-Year Term
Nonsmoker	$11	$14
Smoker	$31	$42

   _____
   _____
   _____
   _____

4. Seth is covered under his employer's health insurance plan and pays 25% of the $412.56 monthly premium. He adds his wife to the insurance plan, but pays 75% of her $412.56 monthly premium. How much is the annual cost of health insurance for Seth and his wife?

   _____
   _____

5. Seth learns about another auto technician job that is available. The wage is $2.50 less per hour. However, this employer offers the same health insurance and pays 100% of the premium for the employee and spouse. Would the better health insurance benefits more than offset the lower hourly wage? Assume that Seth works 40 hours a week.

   _____
   _____

Chapter 12   Insurance

Name _____

6. Seth and his wife have a combined $500 deductible with their health insurance. There is no coinsurance, but they must make a $25 copayment for each visit to their primary care doctor. Copayments do not apply toward the deductible. Seth makes one office visit and his wife makes three. Seth's expenses not covered under his office visit are $414, and his wife's expenses not covered under office visits are $786. How much are their total out-of-pocket expenses?

_____

_____

7. Seth is offered a new health insurance option. He can keep his current plan or he can sign up for a new coinsurance plan. The copayments for the new plan are the same, but the deductible for him and his wife increases to $1,000. In addition, the insurance pays 80% of expenses after the deductible, with a maximum out-of-pocket expense for Seth and his wife of $2,000 (not including copayments). The monthly premium for each employee and dependent is only $327.40. Seth would pay 25% of this premium for himself and 75% for his wife. What is the annual cost of this new plan for Seth and his wife?

_____

_____

8. Suppose Seth and his wife have the same expenses as in question #6. What is the annual cost of this new plan plus the out-of-pocket expenses? How does this compare to the annual cost of their current plan plus the out-of-pocket expenses?

_____

_____

Notes

13 Financial Planning

Name _____ Date _____ Period _____

Part 1: Chapter Review

Multiple Choice

Choose the letter of the correct answer to each question.

1. _____ Inflation is usually estimated using the
   A. gross domestic product.
   B. Consumer Price Index.
   C. present value of an annuity.
   D. future value of an annuity.

2. _____ A will is a legal document that
   A. expresses a person's wishes for his or her estate after death.
   B. identifies the beneficiaries.
   C. names one or more people to manage an estate.
   D. All of the above.

3. _____ The legal process of settling an estate and distributing assets is called
   A. a trust.
   B. probate.
   C. annuitizing.
   D. redistribution.

4. _____ A contribution to an IRA account is
   A. not taxed.
   B. taxed, but at a lower rate than ordinary income.
   C. taxed at the same rate as ordinary income.
   D. allowed in any amount.

5. _____ What happens when there is inflation?
   A. Prices rise and the currency value falls.
   B. Prices fall and the currency value falls.
   C. Prices rise and the currency value rises.
   D. Prices fall and the currency value rises.

6. _____ A 401(k) differs from an IRA because it
   A. requires lower contributions.
   B. prohibits an employer from matching an employee's contribution.
   C. is sponsored by an employer.
   D. All of the above.

7. _____ Which is an example of a revenue-generating asset?
   A. Gold
   B. Rental property
   C. Diamonds
   D. All of the above.

8. _____ How do you calculate a royalty payment?
   A. Amount of sales plus the royalty rate
   B. Amount of sales minus the royalty rate
   C. Amount of sales times the royalty rate
   D. Royalty rate minus total annual expense

9. _____ Which of the following is a way to invest in a business?
   A. Purchase publicly-traded stock.
   B. Start your own business.
   C. Invest in someone else's business.
   D. All of the above.

10. _____ Which of the following is an example of passive income?
   A. Dividend income
   B. Fees from consulting work
   C. Sales commissions
   D. All of the above.

Chapter 13   Financial Planning

Name _____

Fill in the Blank

Using the terms provided, choose the correct answer for each statement.

401(k)
annuity
beneficiaries
inflation
IRA

opportunity cost
passive income
probate
royalties
will

1. Ellen earns _____ from a stock investment, which pay dividends.

2. Ellen buys a(n) _____, which is a type of insurance product used as an investment.

3. Ellen saves money for retirement by contributing $5,000 every year to a(n) _____, which is tax deductible.

4. Ellen is a book author and receives _____ based on the sales of her books.

5. A(n) _____ is a retirement plan sponsored by an employer. In many instances, the employer matches part of the employee's contribution.

6. Ellen wants to grow her savings by more than the _____ rate to maintain buying power.

7. Ellen deposits money in her checking account, which earns very low interest. Her _____ is the income she could have earned from an alternative investment.

8. Ellen has a written _____, which designates how the proceeds of her estate will be distributed when she dies.

9. Ellen designates her brother and sister as _____, who will receive the assets of her estate.

10. A legal process called _____ will settle any debts and claims against Ellen's estate.

Open Response

Answer each of the questions that follow.

1. Why does inflation have a negative effect on building wealth?

   _____
   _____
   _____
   _____

2. How does investing help protect savings from inflation?

   _____
   _____
   _____
   _____

3. Why is it important to have a will?

   _____
   _____
   _____
   _____

4. Identify three sources of retirement income, not including work.

   _____
   _____
   _____
   _____

5. Give three examples of revenue-generating assets.

   _____
   _____
   _____
   _____

Name _____

Part 2: Chapter Activities

Section 13.1 Protecting Wealth

Carey earns $19,000 a year as a customer service representative. She considers leaving her job to attend college full-time to earn an engineering degree. College will cost $20,000 a year.

A. How much will Carey spend to attend college if she earns her degree in four years?

_____

_____

B. What is Carey's opportunity cost to quit her job to attend college?

_____

_____

C. What is Carey's total cost to earn a degree? Include her spending for college plus her opportunity cost.

_____

_____

D. Carey graduates and gets an engineering position with a $58,000 annual salary. How much more does she earn than at her previous job?

_____

_____

E. How many years will Carey need to work after graduation before her additional earnings pay back her total cost to earn her degree?

_____

_____

Section 13.2 Retirement Planning

Lars has decided to contribute to an annuity. He wants the future value of the annuity to be at least $20,000 within no longer than 10 years.

A. Suppose Lars contributes $125 per month for 10 years. If the annuity earns 5% annual interest, what will be the future value of the annuity at the end of the 10-year period? Will this annuity allow Lars to achieve his goal?

_____
_____
_____

B. Suppose the annuity has a 7% interest rate. What will be the future value of the annuity at the end of the 10-year period? How much more income will Lars have at the end of the 10-year period with the higher interest rate? Will this annuity allow Lars to achieve his goal?

_____
_____
_____

C. Suppose the annuity has a 5% interest rate. Lars contributes $300 per month for 5 years. What will be the future value of the annuity at the end of the 5-year period? Will this annuity allow Lars to achieve his goal? Why might Lars choose this annuity rather than a 10-year annuity?

_____
_____
_____

D. Lars participates in a 401(k) plan sponsored by his employer. His annual salary is $64,200. His contribution is 6% of his annual salary. His employer matches his contributions up to 3% of his salary. What is the total amount contributed to the plan for the year?

_____
_____
_____

Name _____

Section 13.3 Other Investments

Jordan receives rental income from three houses. The following table shows information on the income and expenses for the houses.

Description	House A	House B	House C
Monthly rent	$800	$1,000	$1,100
Monthly mortgage	$239	$498	$703
Annual property tax	$755	$1,002	$1,578
Annual insurance	$702	$888	$930
Annual maintenance	$900	$1,100	$1,200

A. What is the net annual income for each rental house? What will be the net annual income of each house after the mortgage is paid off?

_____

_____

_____

B. Jordan has a patent on a bicycle light, which is manufactured and sold by another company under license. Under the terms of the deal, Jordan receives a royalty of $1.55 for each of the first 5,000 lights sold every year. He then receives $2.75 for every light sold in excess of 5,000. How much will Jordan earn in royalties if 3,300 lights are sold in a year? How much will he earn if 13,700 are sold?

_____

_____

Part 3: Project-Based Activity

Crystal is 30 years old, single, and earns $45,200 a year as a sales representative for a medical supplies company. She enrolls in her employer's 401(k) plan to save for retirement. Crystal can contribute a maximum $17,000 annually, which her employer will match up to 4% of her annual salary.

1. Crystal contributes $4,000 a year. What is her employer's matching contribution? What is the total amount contributed each year?

2. Assume Crystal contributes $4,000 each year, her employer contributes 4% of her salary, and the 401(k) investment earns 5% annual interest. How much will she have in her 401(k) when she retires at age 60?

3. Instead of contributing $4,000 each year to her 401(k), Crystal only contributes $1,000. She spends the other $3,000 on vacations and entertainment. How much will she have at age 60 when she retires, assuming her 401(k) earns 5.0%?

4. When Crystal retires, what is the opportunity cost of contributing only $1,000 each year to her 401(k) instead of $4,000? (Ignore tax considerations in your answer.)

5. Crystal earns 5.0% on her 401(k) in the first year she participates. A year ago the CPI was 225.9. Today it is 233.8. Did her investment keep up with inflation?